CONTENTS

CHAPTER 1

INTRODUCTION

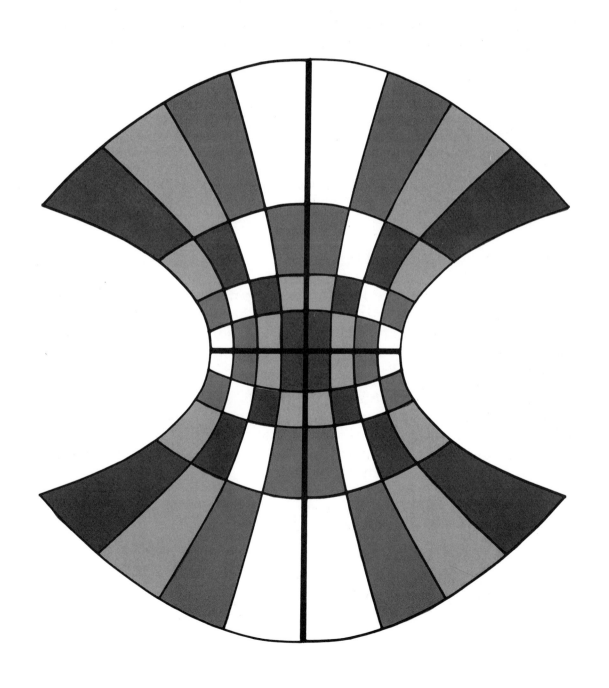

Mathematical patterns occur in every aspect of number relationships: the arithmetic operations exhibit many patterns, or predictable associations, between numbers; a number itself may exhibit a pattern, as in the instance of the repeating decimal; special sequences of numbers, such as the Fibonacci sequence, are mathematical patterns that display many interesting properties. In each area of mathematics, patterns can be found. Indeed, mathematics is the study of pattern.

One of the ways in which we may use number patterns is in the creation of unique and pleasing design. In this book, we will explore several basic techniques through which mathematical patterns form the actual structure of design. These techniques vary in approach and in resulting design, but all mathematical pattern designs share one important feature: they are as consistent and yet as varied as mathematics itself.

MATHEMATICS AND DESIGN CONCEPTS

Before we introduce the designs that will be constructed in each of the succeeding chapters, let us review four concepts that will appear throughout the book: modular arithmetic, transformations, symmetry, and coloring patterns.

MODULAR ARITHMETIC

Arithmetic operations produce many mathematical patterns that can be used in creating design. In modular or clock arithmetic, we work with a finite set of whole numbers determined by the modulo together with the four operations: addition, subtraction, multiplication, and division.

For example, in modulo 3 (also called mod 3), we use the *three* whole numbers 0, 1, and 2. These are the only three elements in the system, and these are the only three numbers that can result from any arithmetic operation. The operations can easily be demonstrated on a clock, marked in mod 3, as in Figure 1-1.

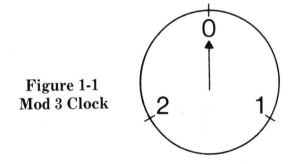

**Figure 1-1
Mod 3 Clock**

Designs From
Mathematical Patterns

Stanley Bezuszka   Margaret Kenney   Linda Silvey

Creative Publications
Palo Alto, CA

Editor   Lyn Savage

Illustrator   Ed Almazol

© 1978 Creative Publications, Inc.
P. O. Box 10328
Palo Alto, California 94303
Printed in U.S.A.

4 5 6 7 8 9 10 . 8 9 8 7 6 5   ISBN: 0-88488-105-9

PREFACE

Symmetries, designs, and patterns surround us from our earliest days. Nature's symmetries in the grasses of the field, the trees of the forest, and the coloring of the various forms of sea life are among our first observations. Nature's patterns were recognized and used by early man. The mysterious patterns of the stars in the night sky were studied by the tillers of the soil and the wayfarers on the seas and oceans of the earth. From the crude markings in the caves of our ancestors to the latest and most complex paintings, mosaics, tilings, and tessellations, we can see that man has strived to express himself in symmetries, designs, and patterns.

Wherever there are patterns, you will find mathematics. Wherever there is mathematics, you will find patterns. This book is an adventure in the application of mathematics to design. In it, we attempt to give the students some personal experience with, as well as enjoyment of, mathematical patterns. The patterns can be readily comprehended and translated into design. The mathematics used is a blend of arithmetic and geometry.

The book is constructed for flexible use. It can serve as the textbook for an independent instructional unit or it can supplement and enrich the classroom text. The activities in the book can be used with students from upper elementary school through high school. In fact, this book provides ample opportunity for each student to develop imagination, insight, and intuition—qualities that mark the healthy and alert mind.

The materials needed for the activities in this book can easily be obtained. These include: copies of the various grids and dot arrays provided in the Appendix; cardboard or tagboard; pencils, pens (especially felt tips), colored pencils, crayons, and paints; scissors, glue, mirrors, and a protractor.

Many activities will be stimulating for those who enjoy embroidery, needlepoint, patchwork quilts, and other crafts. We expect that the creative reader will be motivated to explore his or her own ideas after completing some of the activities.

We hope you enjoy doing the activities as much as we have enjoyed putting them together for you.

Stanley Bezuszka, Margaret Kenney, and Linda Silvey

The hand starts at 0, 1, or 2 and moves around the face of the clock; the direction is determined by the operation and the number of spaces is determined by the numbers used. The number on which the hand stops is the answer to the computation.

Figure 1-2 shows the computation of 1 + 2 in mod 3. The hand starts at 1 and, since we are adding 2 to this number, moves 2 spaces in a clockwise direction. The resulting position is 0. Thus, 1 + 2 = 0 in mod 3.

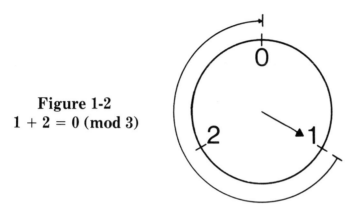

Figure 1-2
1 + 2 = 0 (mod 3)

Using the mod 3 clock face to perform the additions, verify the addition facts given in the table in Figure 1-3.

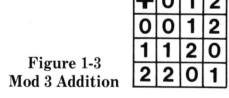

Figure 1-3
Mod 3 Addition

+	0	1	2
0	0	1	2
1	1	2	0
2	2	0	1

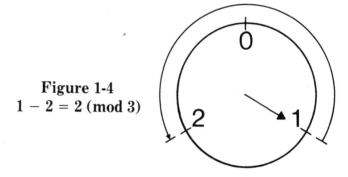

Figure 1-4
1 − 2 = 2 (mod 3)

Since subtraction and addition are inverse operations, subtraction can be performed on the clock by simply moving the hand in a counter-clockwise direction. Figure 1-4 demonstrates the computation of 1 − 2 in mod 3.

Starting at 1, the hand moves 2 spaces in a counterclockwise direction, stopping at 2. In mod 3, 1 − 2 = 2.

Subtraction computations may also be performed directly from the addition table, since $a - b = c$ if and only if $b + c = a$. Using the mod 3 addition table in Figure 1-5, we can compute 1 − 2 in mod 3 as follows: if $1 - 2 = c$, then $2 + c = 1$. Looking in the row headed by the number 2, we find the sum 1 and see what number heads that column.

The addition table tells us that 2 + 2 = 1. Converting this back into our first equation, we find that 1 − 2 = 2.

Check the subtractions in the mod 3 table shown in Figure 1-6. Read the entries "row number minus column number."

+	0	1	2
0	0	1	2
1	1	2	0
2	2	0	1

Figure 1-5
Mod 3 Addition

−	0	1	2
0	0	2	1
1	1	0	2
2	2	1	0

Figure 1-6
Mod 3 Subtraction

Multiplication may be thought of as repeated addition, and modular multiplication is performed in exactly this way. In mod 3, 2 × 2 = 2 + 2 = 1 (Figure 1-7).

Verify the facts in the mod 3 multiplication table in Figure 1-8. The zero row and column are frequently omitted from the multiplication table because the product of any number and zero is always zero.

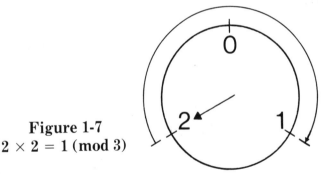

Figure 1-7
2 × 2 = 1 (mod 3)

×	1	2
1	1	2
2	2	1

Figure 1-8
Mod 3 Multiplication

Division is the inverse operation of multiplication. Just as multiplication may be thought of as repeated addition, division may be thought of as subtraction that is repeated until an answer of zero is reached.

Consider the division problem 1 ÷ 2 in mod 3. On the mod 3 clock in Figure 1-9, begin at 1 and subtract 2 repeatedly (moving counter-clockwise) until you reach an answer of 0. The number of times you must subtract 2 before reaching 0 is the quotient in the division problem. In this example, after 2 is subtracted from 1 *twice*, we reach 0. Hence, 1 ÷ 2 = 2 in mod 3.

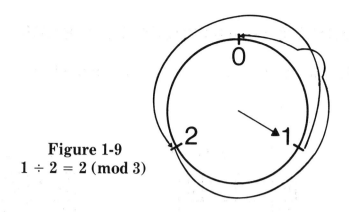

Figure 1-9
$1 \div 2 = 2 \pmod 3$

Solutions to a division problem may also be computed directly from the multiplication table. We know that $a \div b = c$ if and only if $b \times c = a$. Therefore, in the previous example, $1 \div 2 = c$ if and only if $2 \times c = 1$. The mod 3 multiplication table (Figure 1-10) provides the answer. Looking in the row headed by 2, we find the product 1. The product 1 is in the column headed by the number 2. Thus $2 \times 2 = 1$, or $1 \div 2 = 2$.

Figure 1-10
Mod 3 Multiplication

×	1	2
1	1	2
2	2	1

Check the entries in the mod 3 division table shown in Figure 1-11. Read the table "row number divided by column number."

Figure 1-11
Mod 3 Division

÷	1	2
1	1	2
2	2	1

Although a clock helps in visualizing addition and multiplication in modular arithmetic, it is not necessary for computing. It is faster to use this algorithm to add and multiply:
   a) Do the problem as you would in ordinary arithmetic.
   b) Divide your answer by the mod that you are using.
   c) Your final answer will be the remainder in that quotient.

For example, if we wish to compute $5 + 3$ in mod 6, we follow the three steps of the algorithm: $5 + 3 = 8$; $8 \div 6 = 1$ with a remainder of 2; $5 + 3 = 2 \pmod 6$.

In mod 4, $3 \times 3 = 1$, since $3 \times 3 = 9$, and $9 \div 4 = 2$ with a remainder of 1.

Can you explain why this algorithm works?

ACTIVITY: MODULAR ARITHMETIC TABLES

Complete each of the following operations tables, using modular arithmetic.

1. Mod 4 Addition

+	0	1	2	3
0				
1				
2				
3				

2. Mod 4 Subtraction

−	0	1	2	3
0				
1				
2				
3				

3. Mod 5 Multiplication

✕	1	2	3	4
1				
2				
3				
4				

4. Mod 5 Division

÷	1	2	3	4
1				
2				
3				
4				

5. Mod 8 Multiplication

✕	1	2	3	4	5	6	7
1							
2							
3							
4							
5							
6							
7							

6. Mod 12 Addition

+	0	1	2	3	4	5	6	7	8	9	10	11
0												
1												
2												
3												
4												
5												
6												
7												
8												
9												
10												
11												

TRANSFORMATIONS

Once a basic design has been constructed, it may be extended through three different transformations: translation, rotation, and reflection.

A *translation* of a figure in a plane is a rigid linear shift or slide of the figure in that plane. Each point of the figure moves the same distance along parallel lines (Figure 1-12). The triangle A′B′C′ is a translation of triangle ABC.

Because a translation is a rigid motion, triangle A′B′C′ matches triangle ABC exactly. It is customary to call the figure resulting from a transformation the *image* of the original figure. Thus, triangle A′B′C′ is the image of triangle ABC under this translation.

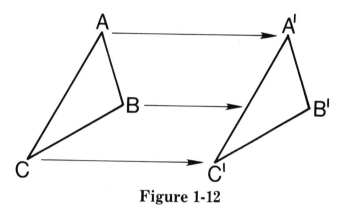

Figure 1-12

A *rotation* of a figure in a plane is a turning of the figure about a given point in the plane called the *center of rotation*. In Figure 1-13, triangle XYZ has been rotated about the point X to a new position in the plane. Point X is the center of rotation. The center of rotation may or may not be in the figure itself. Triangle XY′Z′ is the image of triangle XYZ under this rotation.

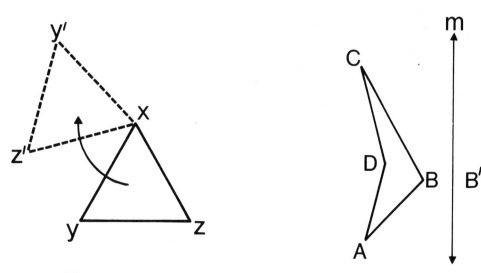

Figure 1-13

Figure 1-14

13

A *reflection* of a figure in a plane is a flipping of the figure over a line called the *line of reflection* or the *mirror line*. In Figure 1-14, the quadrilateral ABCD is reflected over line m. A'B'C'D' is the image of ABCD under this reflection. Notice that ABCD cannot be made to coincide with its reflection A'B'C'D' by any translation or rotation.

It is often simpler to think of a translation as a *slide*, a rotation as a *turn*, and a reflection as a *flip*.

The following are examples of the ways in which a basic design pattern can be extended through transformations.

Basic Design Pattern

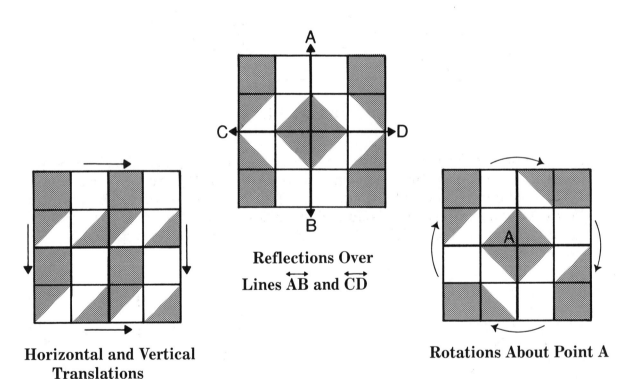

Reflections Over
Lines $\overleftrightarrow{AB}$ and $\overleftrightarrow{CD}$

Horizontal and Vertical Translations

Rotations About Point A

Figure 1-15

Notice how each transformation produces a different extended design from the same basic pattern.

ACTIVITY: TRANSFORMATIONS

A basic design pattern can be extended to form an attractive larger design through translations, rotations, reflections, or combinations of these. Follow the instructions in each problem to extend the basic design patterns to larger areas.

1. Translate or slide the basic pattern to each of the other three squares in the design grid.

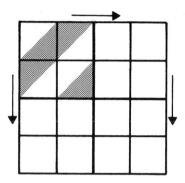

2. Using 90° clockwise rotations or turns about the point O, rotate the basic pattern to each of the other three squares in the design grid.

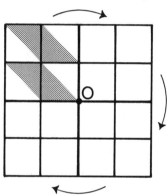

3. Reflect or flip the basic pattern over the line $\overleftrightarrow{AB}$. Then reflect the resulting design over line $\overleftrightarrow{CD}$.

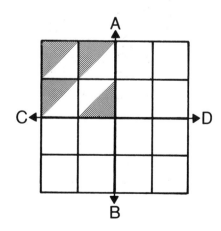

SYMMETRY

One quality of design that is especially pleasing to the eye is symmetry. Two types of symmetry that arise in mathematical pattern designs are line symmetry and rotational symmetry. These are closely related to reflections and rotations. The design in Figure 1-16 has a line of symmetry along the dotted line. The left and right halves of the design are reflections of one another over the line of symmetry. The design in Figure 1-17 has no lines of symmetry, but does have rotational symmetry about its center O. If this design is rotated 180° about its center, it will coincide with itself.

Figure 1-16   **Figure 1-17**

Certain mathematical patterns possess symmetry of their own, and it is because of this that designs created from these patterns will also be symmetric. An illustration of this can be seen in the mod 5 addition table in Figure 1-18. Note the line of symmetry along the diagonal.

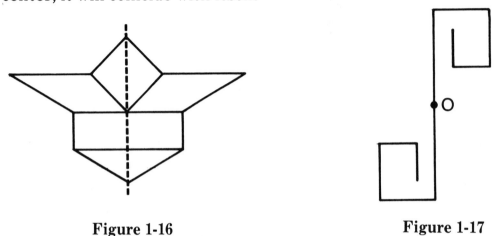

+	0	1	2	3	4
0	0	1	2	3	4
1	1	2	3	4	0
2	2	3	4	0	1
3	3	4	0	1	2
4	4	0	1	2	3

Figure 1-18

Even basic patterns that do not have symmetry can be extended to symmetric designs through reflections and rotations.

16

ACTIVITY: SYMMETRY

1. Draw and letter the lines of symmetry in each design.

2. Describe the rotational symmetry in each design by labeling the turn center O and naming the degree measure(s) of the counter-clockwise turn(s).

Example:

Lines: *m, p, q*

Turns: 120°, 240°, 360°

Lines: _____

Turns: _____

Lines: _____

Turns: _____

Lines: _____

Turns: _____

Lines: _____

Turns: _____

Lines: _____

Turns: _____

Lines: _____

Turns: _____

Lines: _____

Turns: _____

17

COLORING PATTERNS

To construct the designs in Chapters 2 through 4, we will use mathematical patterns to determine a coloring pattern within a geometric grid. In some of the designs, we will assign a certain color to each number in the pattern, and will color the grid according to that color code (Figure 1-19).

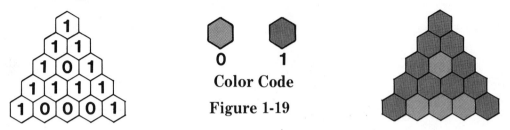

Color Code

Figure 1-19

In other designs, particularly in those designs that use square grids, we will assign a patterned-square design to each number of the pattern, and will color the grid according to that design code (Figure 1-20). To create patterned-square designs, we divide a given square into eight equal regions, and color in some of the eight regions. Figure 1-21 shows some examples of patterned-square designs.

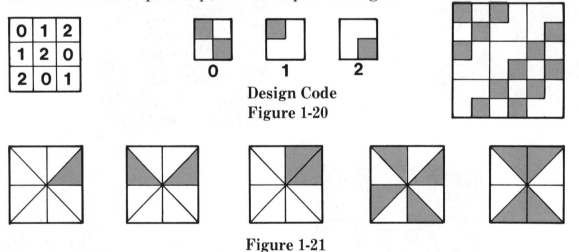

Design Code
Figure 1-20

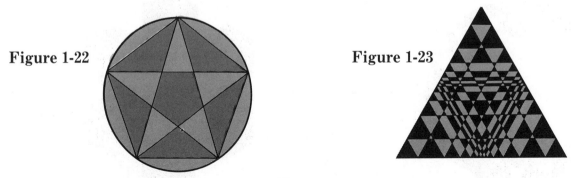

Figure 1-21

For constructing the designs in Chapters 5 through 8, we will use coloring to enhance the design structure created by mathematical pattern. One common rule for coloring such designs is as follows: No two adjacent regions may be the same color. Figures 1-22 and 1-23 illustrate this type of coloring.

Figure 1-22

Figure 1-23

18

ACTIVITY: COLORING PATTERNS

Consider a square separated into eight regions of equal area. Each of the eight regions contains one-eighth of the area of the entire square. If *two* of the eight regions are colored with one color, it is a *quarter-coloring*. If *four* of the regions are colored with one color, it is a *half-coloring*. Two coloring patterns are considered alike if one of them is a reflection and/or a rotation of the other.

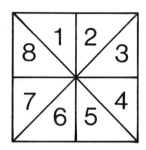

1. Find six different quarter-colorings.

2. Find 13 different half-colorings.

3. Color this design so that no two adjacent regions are the same color.

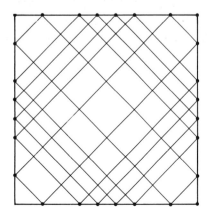

19

DESIGN CONSTRUCTION TECHNIQUES

In this book, two approaches to creating mathematical pattern designs are taken. In one approach, a geometric design (usually a tessellation of geometric shapes) is chosen first, and the mathematical pattern is used to produce a design of colors or patterned squares within the geometric outline. In the second approach, the mathematical pattern is used to dictate the geometric construction of the design, and coloring or shading is added to emphasize the artistry of the mathematical pattern design.

It is important to note that in the first approach (interior design), the mathematical pattern dictates the colors and patterned-square designs within a random exterior form; while in the second approach (exterior design), the mathematical pattern dictates the exterior form of the design, and the color and other internal markings are chosen randomly. Both approaches produce intriguing design; both approaches allow for flexibility and creativity.

In the following three chapters, we will discover several different methods of interior design construction, and the ways in which these constructions may be extended into a complete design. In the last four chapters, we will use some of the same methods, and some new ones, to create exterior designs from mathematical patterns.

INTERIOR DESIGN

Chapter 2 explores the tabular patterns produced by the four arithmetic operations in various mods, and the designs that can be created by these tabular patterns. Tabular patterns are those that can be written in the form of a table or a grid.

Once the mod and operation are chosen, and the table completed, a color or patterned square is assigned to each distinct number of the table. Each number is then replaced by its corresponding color or design. For example, if all 2's in a mod 3 addition table are assigned the color red, each square marked 2 in the table is colored red. This produces a basic design pattern, which is extended through transformations. Further variety is achieved through the distortion of the table, or grid. Figures 1-24 and 1-25 are results of this type of interior design construction.

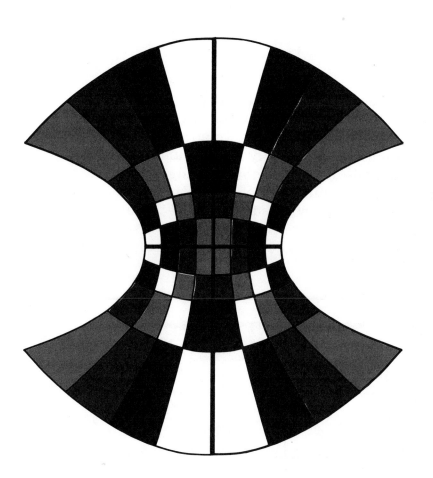

Figure 1-24

Figure 1-25

This process of creating interior design is expanded to include other tabular patterns in Chapter 3. Designs in this chapter are constructed by using tabular patterns formed by latin squares. In a latin square, the mathematical pattern is produced differently than in an arithmetic operations table, but the method of filling in the basic design pattern and transforming it are the same. The numbers of the pattern are replaced by corresponding colors or patterned squares, and the basic design pattern is extended to a larger grid through translations, rotations, or reflections. An illustration of a design created from a latin square is shown in Figure 1-26.

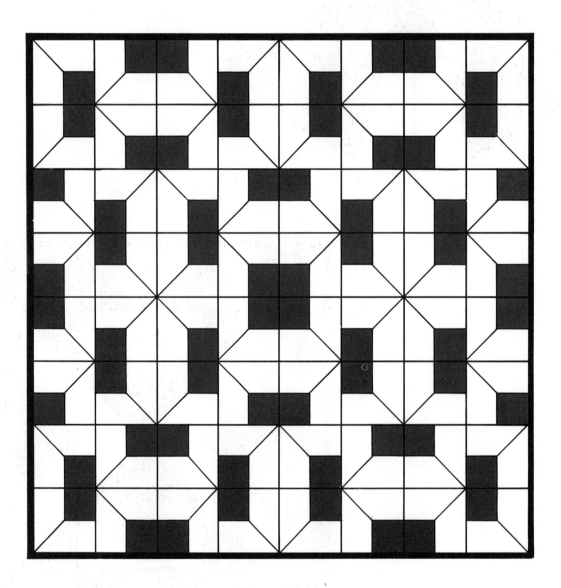

Figure 1-26

In Chapter 4, the same technique is applied to a much different type of tabular pattern: Pascal's triangle. Modular arithmetic is used to generate a finite number of elements, and the pattern of Pascal's triangle dictates the way in which these elements are combined. The elements are again transferred onto a triangular geometric grid or tessellation (the grid must be appropriate to allow for diagonal addition) and then replaced by colors. This grid is rotated about its apex to produce the completed design (Figure 1-27).

Figure 1-27

EXTERIOR DESIGN

Chapter 5 uses modular arithmetic in the construction of circular designs. Star polygons are created by placing equally spaced numbered points on a circle and then connecting the points in an order determined by a modular addition pattern. Product designs are constructed in a similar manner, with the sequence of points determined by a modular multiplication pattern. As a final step, coloring is used to enhance the beauty of these designs. Examples of this type of exterior construction can be seen in Figures 1-28 and 1-29.

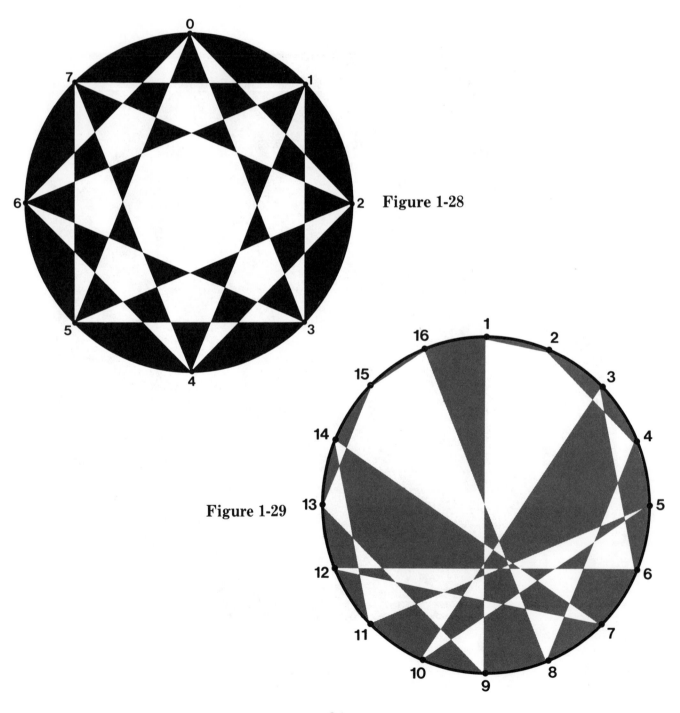

Figure 1-28

Figure 1-29

In Chapter 6, the tabular pattern of the magic square is used to construct exterior design. In Chapter 2, the numbers of the table are replaced by patterned-square designs; in this chapter, the numbers are placed on a square dot array and the dots are then connected in numerical order. These basic design patterns created from magic squares can also be extended through transformations, just as the designs in Chapters 2 and 3 were. Figure 1-30 shows a magic square design that has been extended and shaded.

Figure 1-30

The Fibonacci sequence of numbers is used in Chapter 7 to create many interesting designs (Figure 1-31). The sides of a polygon are divided into sections corresponding in length to the numbers in the sequence, and the points of division are connected to form a grid, which is then shaded or colored in. These polygonal designs can be used in complex tessellation patterns, tangram puzzles, or polyhedra construction.

Figure 1-31

Spirograms—spirals formed by straight line segments—are examined in Chapter 8. The mathematical patterns that create these external designs are infinite number sequences—counting numbers, even numbers, odd numbers, Fibonacci numbers.

A given number sequence determines the length of successive line segments and the order in which they are to be joined. Then an angle measure is chosen and the line segments are connected in order, each successive line being turned according to the angle measure.

This method of creating spirograms is easy to learn and use, but the results are especially fascinating because all types of spirograms can be constructed. Some of the spirograms are simple, some intricate. Some repeat themselves, and are closed while some never close. Every number sequence and every angle measure produces a different and unexpected design (Figures 1-32 and 1-33).

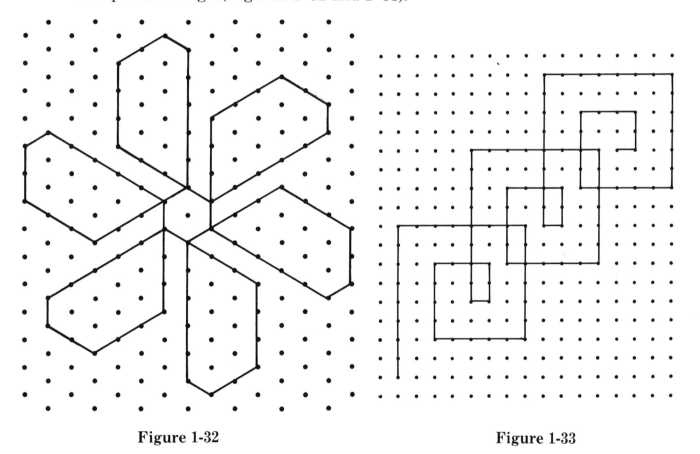

Figure 1-32   Figure 1-33

The methods of design construction that will be presented in this book are intended to be simple and fun to work with. Each chapter offers a new approach and many new designs that can be created.

The methods given are intended to spark the imagination, so that each chapter may become a starting point from which you will explore many more designs from mathematical patterns.

CHAPTER 2

TABULAR DESIGNS FROM MODULAR ARITHMETIC OPERATIONS

MODULAR OPERATIONS TABLES AND COLOR PATTERNS

There are many ways to create basic design patterns from modular arithmetic operations tables. Perhaps the simplest of these is to assign colors to the numbers in a particular table. Figures 2-1 through 2-3 illustrate how we can do this.

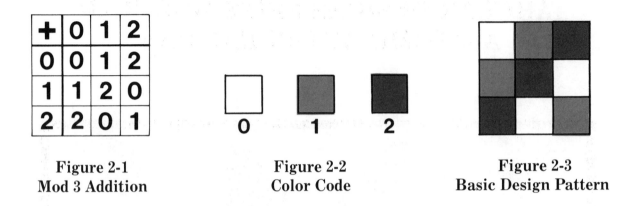

Figure 2-1
Mod 3 Addition

Figure 2-2
Color Code

Figure 2-3
Basic Design Pattern

Figure 2-1 shows the mod 3 addition table. Notice that the interior of the table is a 3 × 3 grid of squares. We assign the following colors to the numbers of the mod 3 table: white to 0, gray to 1, and black to 2 (Figure 2-2). We then color each square of the table according to the number marked in it. Figure 2-3 shows the pattern that results from this coloring.

We can now use this combination of nine squares as a basic design pattern, which we can translate, reflect, or rotate to form larger, more artistic designs. First we copy this basic design pattern in one of the four corners of a 6 × 6 grid. (In Figure 2-4, the basic pattern has been copied in the upper left corner, which will be called *location 1*.) To finish the 6 × 6 design, we copy the pattern from location 1 in locations 2, 3, and 4 through translation, reflection, or rotation in any order to each new location. One possibility is shown in Figure 2-5. Can you describe how it was completed?

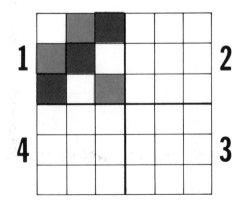

Figure 2-4

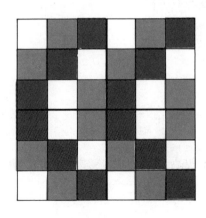

Figure 2-5

ACTIVITY: MOD 4 ADDITION

1. Complete the mod 4 addition table.

+	0	1	2	3
0				
1				
2				
3				

2. Assign a different color to each of the numbers 0, 1, 2, and 3.

    ☐   ☐   ☐   ☐
    0   1   2   3

3. Substituting colors for numbers, copy the interior of the addition table in the upper left corner (location 1) of the 8 × 8 grid below. This is the basic design pattern. Location 1 is the starting position.

4. Complete the design of the 8 × 8 grid by repeating the basic design pattern in locations 2, 3, and 4. (This is the same as translating or sliding the basic pattern to locations 2, 3, and 4.)

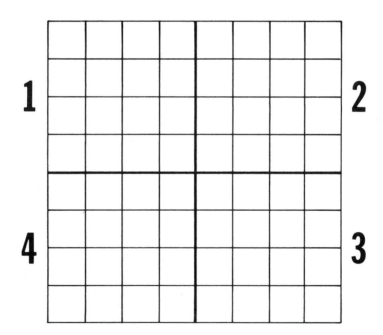

Extensions

1. On copies of page A-1, make other 8 × 8 designs by: (a) reflecting or flipping the basic pattern onto locations 2, 3, and 4; and (b) rotating or turning the basic pattern to locations 2, 3, and 4. Compare these designs with the first design.

2. Use the mod 5 multiplication table to create an 8 × 8 design on another copy of page A-1.

ACTIVITY: MOD 4 SUBTRACTION

1. Complete the mod 4 subtraction table.

−	0	1	2	3
0				
1				
2				
3				

2. Assign a different color to each of the numbers 0, 1, 2, and 3.

☐   ☐   ☐   ☐
0   1   2   3

3. Substituting the colors for the numbers, copy the interior of the subtraction table in the upper left corner (location 1) of the 8 × 8 grid below. Location 1 is the starting position.

4. Reflect or flip the pattern from location 1 onto locations 2, 3, and 4 in any order to complete the coloring of the 8 × 8 design.

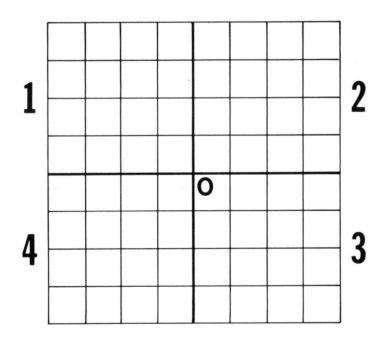

Extension

On a copy of page A-1, rotate the basic design pattern from location 1 in successive 90° turns about the center O to locations 2, 3, and 4. Compare this design with the first design.

ACTIVITY: MOD 8 MULTIPLICATION

1. Complete the partial mod 8 multiplication table.

✗	1	3	5	7
1				
3				
5				
7				

2. The 4 × 4 grid of squares can be distorted as shown below. Copy the interior of the mod 8 multiplication table in this distorted grid. Some numbers have already been placed for you.

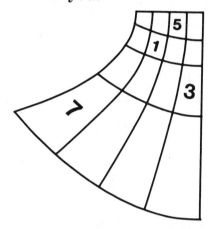

3. Assign a different color to each of the numbers 1, 3, 5, and 7.

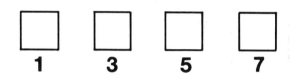

4. Substituting colors for numbers, copy the interior of the distorted grid in the lower left corner (location 1) of the 8 × 8 grid below. Reflect or flip the basic pattern onto locations 2, 3, and 4 to complete the coloring of the 8 × 8 design.

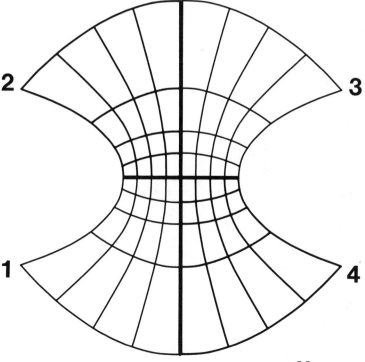

33

ACTIVITY: MOD 5 DIVISION

1. Complete the mod 5 division table.

÷	1	2	3	4
1				
2				
3				
4				

2. Copy the interior of the mod 5 division table in the distorted 4 × 4 grid.

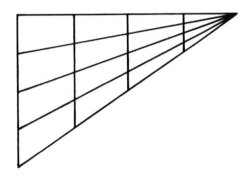

3. Assign a different color to each of the numbers 1, 2, 3, and 4.

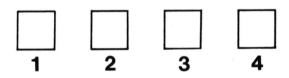

4. Substituting the colors for the numbers, copy the interior of the distorted grid in the lower right corner (location 1) of the 8 × 8 grid. Location 1 is the starting position.

5. Reflect or flip the pattern from location 1 onto locations 2, 3, and 4 to complete the coloring of the 8 × 8 design.

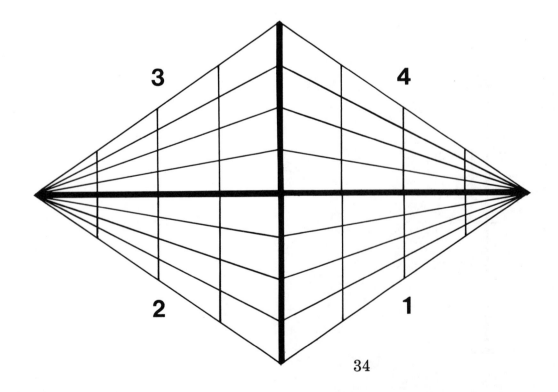

MODULAR OPERATIONS TABLES AND DESIGN PATTERNS

Another way to create basic design patterns from modular arithmetic operations is to assign a patterned square to each number in the interior of a table. Figures 2-6 through 2-8 illustrate how we can do this.

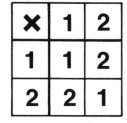

Figure 2-6
Mod 3 Multiplication

Figure 2-7
Design Code

Figure 2-8
Basic Design Pattern

Figure 2-6 shows the mod 3 multiplication table. We begin by assigning patterned squares to the numbers of the mod 3 table (Figure 2-7). Then we fill each square of the table with a pattern according to the number marked in it. Figure 2-8 shows the basic design pattern that results from the patterned squares.

We can now translate, reflect, or rotate this combination of four squares to form larger, more complex designs. First we copy this basic design pattern in one of the four corners of a 4 × 4 grid. (In Figure 2-9, the lower right corner has been used as location 1.) To finish the 4 × 4 design, we copy the pattern from location 1 in locations 2, 3, and 4 using transformations. The 4 × 4 design in Figure 2-10 is the result of the translation, reflection, or rotation of the basic design pattern to locations 2, 3, and 4 in some order. Can you describe how Figure 2-10 was drawn?

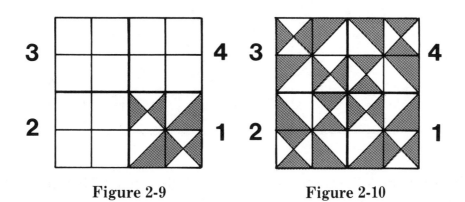

Figure 2-9   **Figure 2-10**

35

ACTIVITY: MOD 4 MULTIPLICATION

1. Complete the mod 4 multiplication table.

✖	0	1	2	3
0				
1				
2				
3				

2. Let 0, 1, 2, and 3 be represented by the designs below.

   0   1   2   3

3. Substituting the designs for the numbers, copy the interior of the multiplication table in the upper left corner (location 1) of the 8 × 8 grid.

4. Reflect or flip the pattern from location 1 onto location 2. Complete the 8 × 8 grid by reflecting the pattern from locations 1 and 2 onto locations 3 and 4.

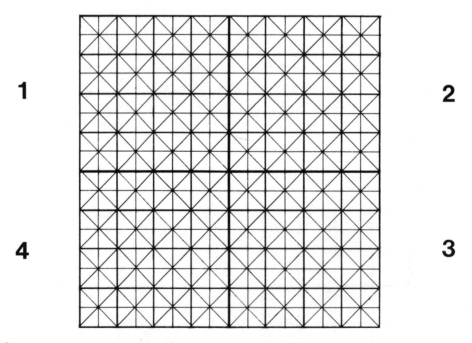

Extensions

On copies of page A-2, create different 8 × 8 designs with combinations of reflections, translations, and rotations. You may wish to change the position of location 1 or to use different colors for the darkened part of the design for each number.

ACTIVITY: MOD 5 ADDITION

1. Complete the mod 5 addition table.

+	0	1	2	3	4
0					
1					
2					
3					
4					

2. Let 0, 1, 2, 3, and 4 be represented by the designs below.

    0   1   2   3   4

3. Substituting the designs for the numbers, copy the interior of the addition table in the upper left corner (location 1) of the 10 × 10 grid.

4. Rotate or turn the pattern from location 1 in successive clockwise 90° turns about the center O to locations 2, 3, and 4.

1   2

O

4   3

37

ACTIVITY: MOD 8 ADDITION

1. Complete the mod 8 addition table.

+	1	2	3	4	5	6	7	0
1								
2								
3								
4								
5								
6								
7								
0								

2. Let 0, 1, 2, 3, 4, 5, 6, and 7 be represented by the designs below.

 0   1   2   3 4

5   6   7

3. Substituting the designs for the numbers, copy the interior of the addition table in the upper left corner (location 1) of the 16 × 16 grid below.

4. Reflect or flip the pattern from location 1 onto locations 2, 3, and 4 in any order to complete the 16 × 16 design.

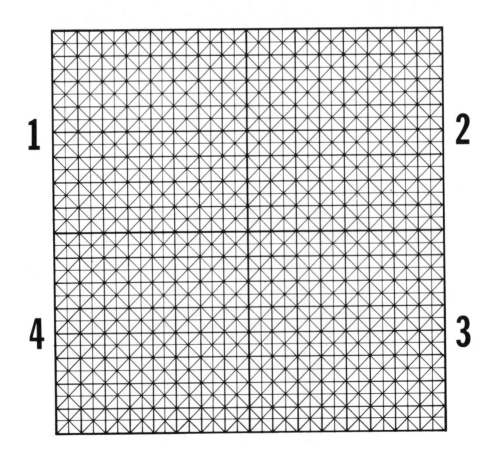

ACTIVITY: MOD 4 ADDITION

1. Complete the mod 4 addition table.

+	0	1	2	3
0				
1				
2				
3				

2. The 4 × 4 grid of squares can be distorted as shown below. Copy the interior of the mod 4 addition table in this distorted grid.

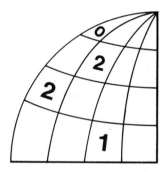

3. Select four different colors.

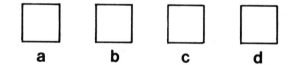

Color each numbered region according to the letters marked in it.

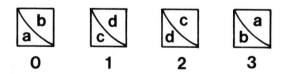

4. Substituting the designs for the numbers, copy the interior of the distorted grid in the upper left corner (location 1) of the 8 × 8 grid on the following page.

5. Complete the design by reflecting the pattern from location 1 onto locations 2, 3, and 4.

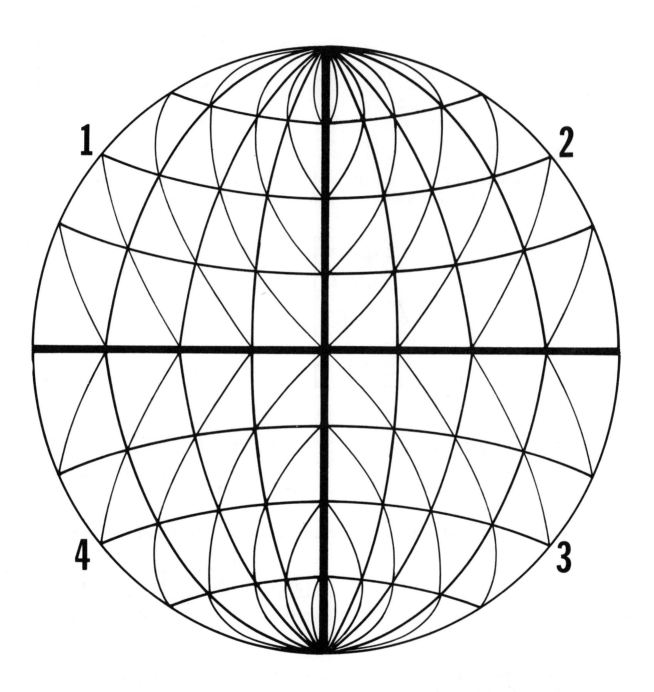

ACTIVITY: MOD 6 ADDITION

1. Complete the mod 6 addition table.

+	0	1	2	3	4	5
0						
1						
2						
3						
4						
5						

2. The 6 × 6 grid of squares can be distorted as shown below. Copy the interior of the mod 6 addition table in this distorted grid.

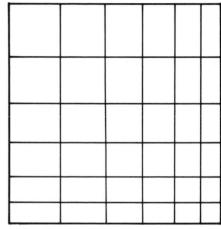

3. Select three different colors.

   a   b   c

Color each numbered region according to the letters marked in it.

  0   1   2   3   4   5

4. Substituting the designs for the numbers, copy the interior of the addition table in the upper left corner (location 1) of the 12 × 12 grid on the following page.

5. Complete the design by reflecting the basic design pattern from location 1 onto locations 2, 3, and 4.

Extensions

1. On a duplicate of the following page or page A-3, copy the same basic design pattern in location 1. Rotate the pattern in successive 90° clockwise turns about the center O to complete the 12 × 12 design. Are the two 12 × 12 designs the same? Why or why not?

41

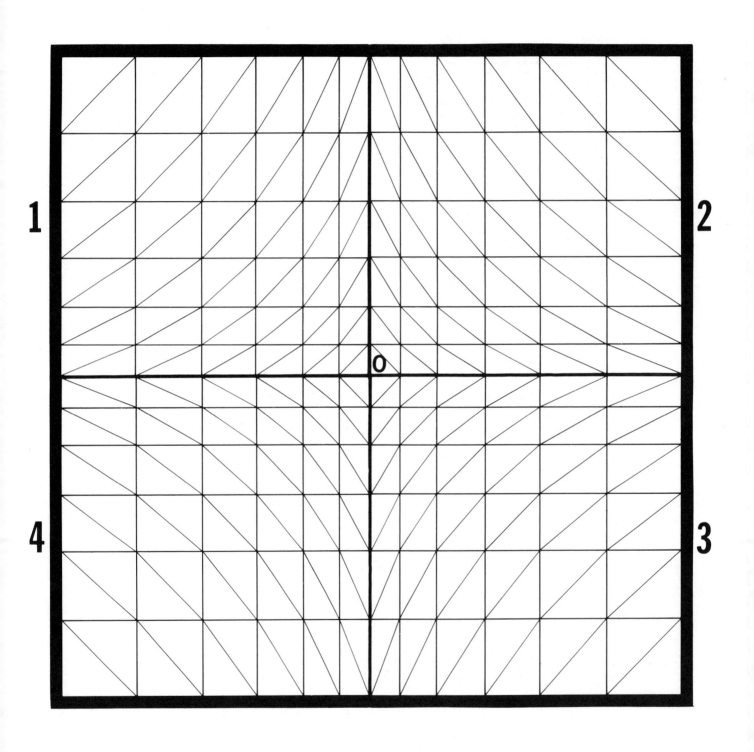

ACTIVITY: MOD 12 ADDITION

1. Complete the partial mod 12 addition tables.

+	0	2	4	6	8	10
0						
2						
4						
6						
8						
10						

+	2	4	6	8	10	0
2						
4						
6						
8						
10						
0						

2. Copy the interior of the partial mod 12 addition tables in the distorted 6 × 6 grids.

A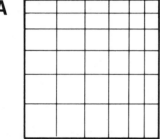

B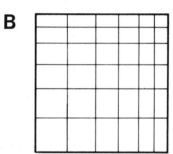

3. Select three different colors.

a   b   c

Color each numbered region according to the letters marked in it.

0   2   4   6   8   10

4. Substituting the designs for the numbers, copy the interior of the addition table (A) in the upper left corner (location 1) of the 12 × 12 grid on the following page.

5. Complete the 12 × 12 design by rotating the basic design pattern from location 1 in successive 90° turns about center O.

6. On a copy of the following page or page A-4, substitute the designs for the numbers and copy the interior of the addition table (B) in the upper left corner (location 1) of the 12 × 12 grid.

7. Complete the 12 × 12 design by rotating the basic design pattern from location 1 in successive 90° turns about center O. Compare the two finished 12 × 12 designs.

43

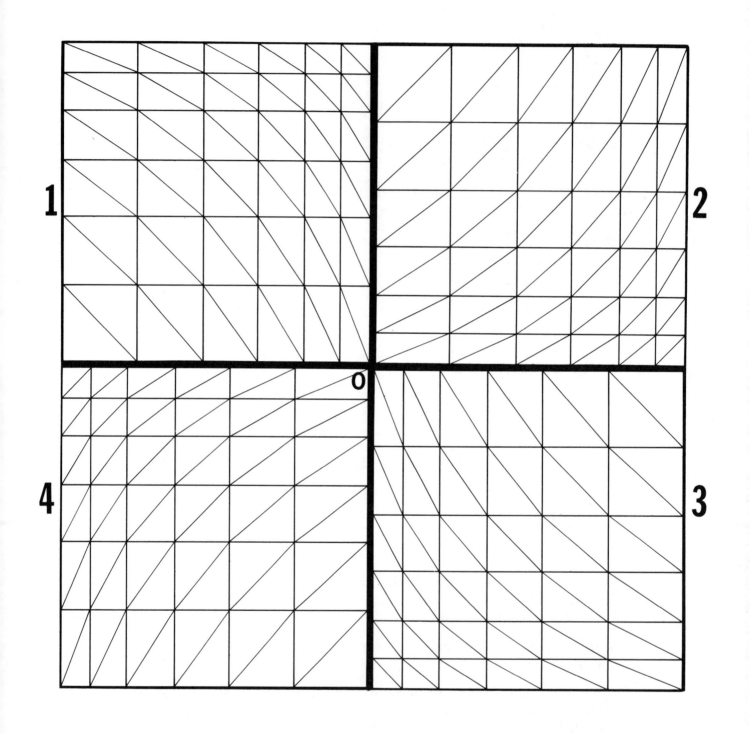

ACTIVITY: MOD 16 MULTIPLICATION

1. Complete the partial mod 16 multiplication table.

✖	1	7	9	15
1				
7				
9				
15				

2. Copy the interior of the partial mod 16 multiplication table in the distorted 4 × 4 grid below.

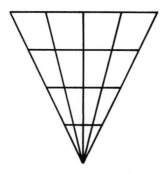

3. Select two different colors.

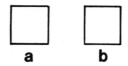

    a   b

Color each numbered region according to the letters marked in it.

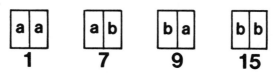

4. Substituting the designs for the numbers, copy the interior of the multiplication table in the triangular location 1 of the hexagonal grid on the following page.

5. Using 60° turns only, extend the basic design pattern from location 1 to locations 2, 3, 4, 5, and 6 to complete the coloring of the hexagonal design.

Extension

On a copy of the following page or page A-5, complete a hexagonal design based on reflections only, starting with the same triangular location 1. Are both your designs the same?

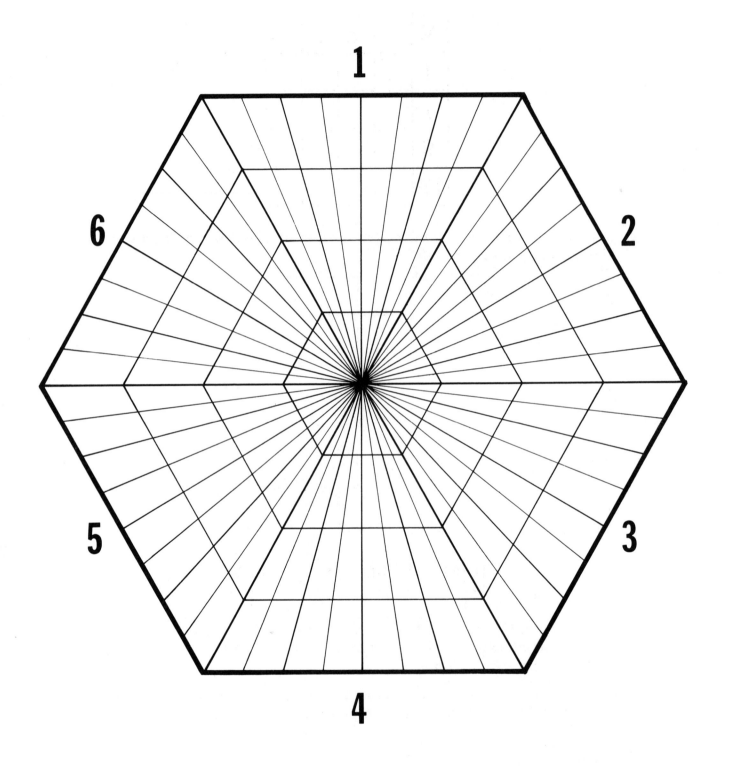

SUMMARY: MAKING GRIDS AND MOD DESIGNS

1. Take a starting grid such as this one.

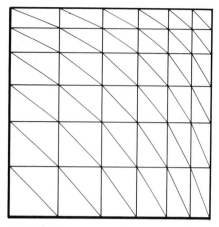

Use some combination of reflections, rotations, and translations to form a 12 × 12 grid. One example is given below. Construct some others, and then try to develop grids of other sizes in a similar manner (such as a 10 × 10 and a 16 × 16 grid).

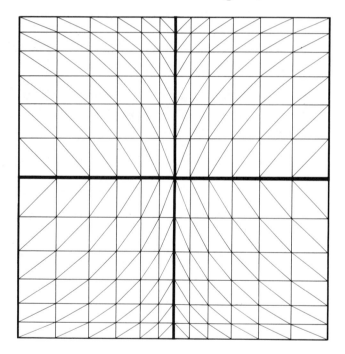

2. Select an appropriate mod and operation, and complete a table for them.

3. Decide how many colors you want to include in your design. Assign these colors to the numbered regions as in the preceding activities.

4. Fill in the section of the grid that you designate as location 1, substituting your choice of colors for the numbers. Then by translations, reflections, and rotations, extend the design to locations 2, 3, and 4.

Have fun creating your own original designs.

ADDITIONAL ACTIVITIES

Pages A-1 to A-8 of the Appendix are blank grids which you may use for creating tabular designs from modular arithmetic tables and transformations (translations, reflections, and rotations). Though specifically intended for 12 × 12 tabular designs, the grids on pages A-7 and A-8 are distortions of the standard grid. Once the pattern for location 1 has been determined, fill in locations 2, 3, and 4 by some choice of translations, rotations, or reflections of the *color* design rather than the shape design.

The suggestions given here are meant to stimulate your imagination and to encourage you to try your own ideas for tables, grids, and designs.

Appendix Page	Modular Arithmetic Table
A-7	Mod 5 multiplication, using numbers 1, 2, 3, 4
A-8	Mod 4 multiplication, using numbers 0, 1, 2, 3
A-8	Mod 5 multiplication, using numbers 0, 1, 2, 3, 4 (Try using pictures of flowers in one or more of the replacements for the numbers to get a patchwork quilt design.)
A-6	Mod 8 division, using numbers 1, 3, 5, 7 (Color this design in a way similar to that used in the activity on page 45.)
A-7	Mod 12 subtraction, using numbers 0, 3, 6, 9
A-6	Mod 8 addition, using numbers 0, 2, 4, 6
A-5	Mod 4 subtraction, using numbers 0, 1, 2, 3

CHAPTER 3

TABULAR DESIGNS FROM LATIN SQUARES

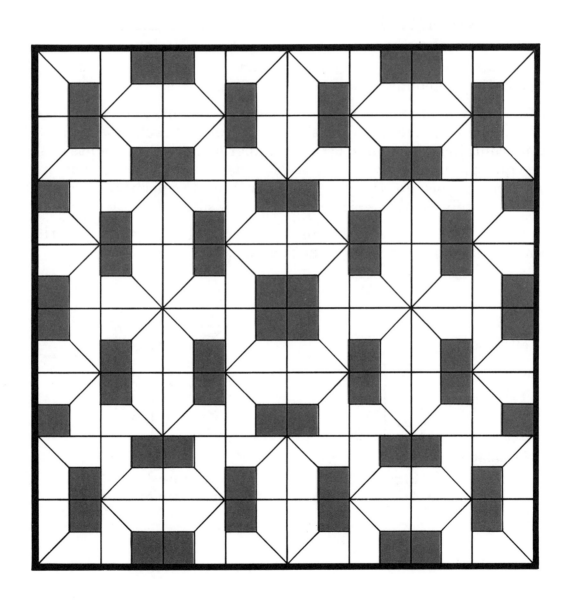

In Chapter 2, we explored some basic design patterns that can be generated from modular arithmetic tables. We also explored ways in which we could create larger designs based on those tabular patterns. We replaced entries in the tables by colors and/or designs to create a basic pattern which we rotated, translated, or reflected to complete the finished design.

In this chapter, we will look at another type of tabular pattern—the latin square— and we will use the technique developed in Chapter 2 to create latin square designs.

LATIN SQUARES

Latin squares were first developed systematically by the Swiss mathematician Leonard Euler (1707−1783).

A *latin square* of order n is a square table of elements such that: (1) the total number of elements in the table equals n^2; (2) each row and column contains n elements; (3) the number of distinct elements in the table equals n; and (4) *each of the* n *elements appears exactly once in any column or row*. For the present, we will use the positive integers 1, 2, 3, . . . n to represent the elements of a latin square.

Figures 3-1 through 3-4 show latin squares of various orders with the two main diagonals marked on each square.

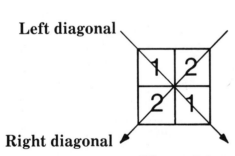

Figure 3-1
Latin Square of Order 2

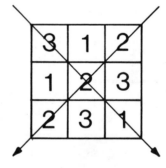

Figure 3-2
Latin Square of Order 3

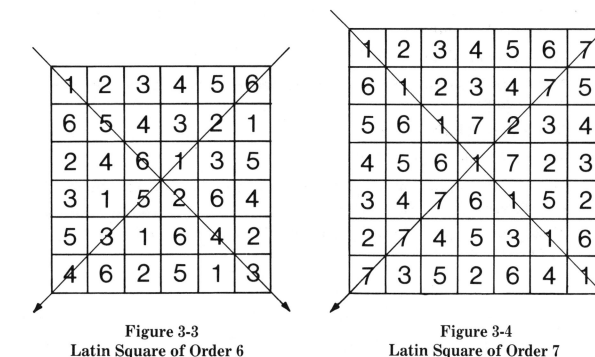

Figure 3-3
Latin Square of Order 6

Figure 3-4
Latin Square of Order 7

A *cross latin square* is a latin square of order n in which all the entries on one diagonal are the same positive integer and all the entries on the other diagonal are the same positive integer. Figure 3-1 shows a cross latin square of order 2. The order of a cross latin square is always an even number n.

A *single diagonal latin square* is a latin square of order n in which each positive integer 1, 2, 3, . . . n occurs exactly once along one of the diagonals. Figure 3-2 shows a single diagonal latin square of order 3.

A *double diagonal latin square* is a latin square of order n in which each positive integer 1, 2, 3, . . . n occurs exactly once on each of the two diagonals. Figure 3-3 shows a double diagonal latin square of order 6.

A diagonal of a latin square is a *line of symmetry* if the corresponding entries on opposite sides of the diagonal are equal. Figure 3-2 is a latin square in which the left diagonal is a line of symmetry.

ACTIVITY: LATIN SQUARES, ORDER 4

Construct six different latin squares of order 4 to satisfy the conditions in problems 1 through 6.

1. Make a single diagonal latin square.

2. Make a latin square in which the elements on the left diagonal are all the same.

3. Make a cross latin square.

4. Make a double diagonal latin square.

5. Make a latin square in which the left diagonal is a line of symmetry for the square.

6. Make a latin square in which the left diagonal is not a line of symmetry for the square.

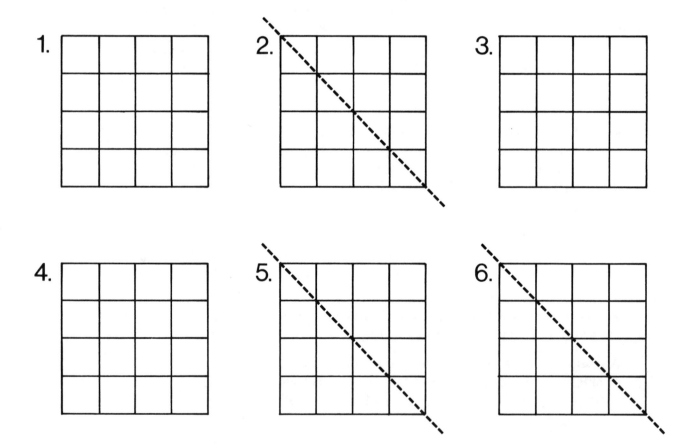

ACTIVITY: LATIN SQUARES, ORDER 5

Construct six different latin squares of order 5 to satisfy the conditions in problems 1 through 6.

1. Make a single diagonal latin square.

2. Make a latin square in which the elements on the right diagonal are all the same.

3. Make a double diagonal latin square.

4. Make a latin square in which the right diagonal is a line of symmetry.

5. Make a latin square in which the right diagonal is not a line of symmetry.

6. Make a latin square in which the first row is the same as the first column and the fifth row is the same as the fifth column.

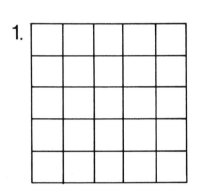 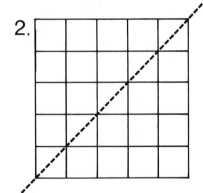 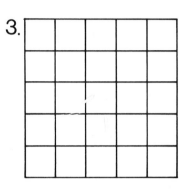

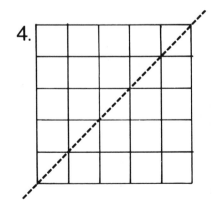 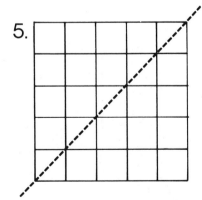 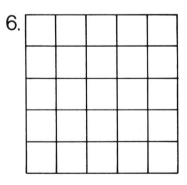

7. Can you make a cross latin square of order 5? _____ Why or why not?

8. Is the interior of the mod 4 multiplication table a latin square of order 4? _____

9. Is the interior of the mod 5 addition table a latin square of order 5? _____

LATIN SQUARE DESIGNS

We can create a latin square design by substituting colors or patterned squares for the numbers in the table. Figures 3-5 through 3-7 illustrate how we can do this.

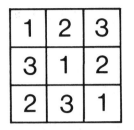

Figure 3-5
Latin Square of Order 3

Figure 3-6
Design Code

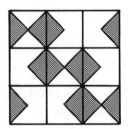

Figure 3-7
Basic Design Pattern

Figure 3-5 shows a latin square of order 3. We assign a patterned square to each of the numbers 1, 2, 3 (Figure 3-6). Then we substitute the patterned squares for the numbers in the latin square. Figure 3-7 shows the basic design pattern that results from the patterned squares.

We can construct many different designs if we translate, reflect, or rotate this basic design pattern to other locations on a 6 x 6 grid. One such 6 x 6 design is shown in Figure 3-8. Can you describe how it was formed?

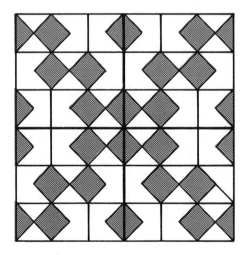

Figure 3-8

What fractional part of the square design is shaded in Figure 3-8?

ACTIVITY: LATIN SQUARE DESIGNS, ORDER 3

1. Assign the numbers 1, 2, 3 in any order to the patterned squares below.

2. Substituting the patterned squares for the numbers in the latin square, fill in the basic design pattern.

1	3	2
3	2	1
2	1	3

Latin Square

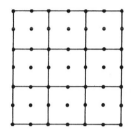

Basic Design Pattern

3. Create a 6 x 6 square design. Copy your basic design pattern in the upper left corner of the 6 x 6 grid. Complete the design by using some combination of translations, reflections, and rotations of the basic pattern. Be able to describe how you completed your design.

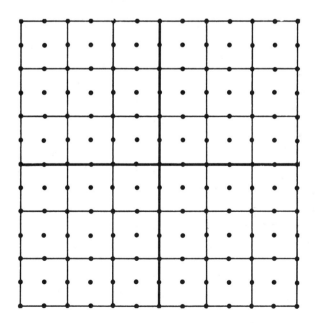

4. What fractional part of your finished design is shaded? _____

ACTIVITY: LATIN SQUARE DESIGNS, ORDER 4

1. Assign the numbers 1, 2, 3, and 4 in any order to the patterned squares below.

    —   —   —   —

2. Substituting the patterned squares for the numbers in the latin square, fill in the basic design pattern.

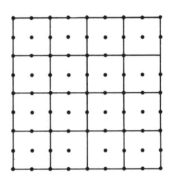

4	3	2	1
3	4	1	2
1	2	3	4
2	1	4	3

Latin Square   **Basic Design Pattern**

3. Create an 8 x 8 square design. Copy your basic design in the upper left corner of the 8 x 8 grid. Complete the design by using some combination of translations, reflections, and rotations of the basic pattern. Be able to describe how you completed your design.

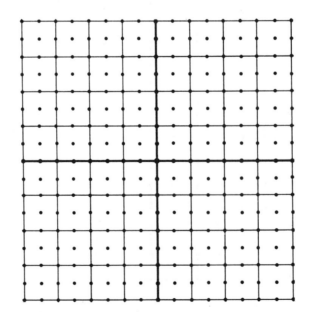

4. What fractional part of your finished design is shaded? _____

56

ACTIVITY: LATIN SQUARE DESIGN, ORDER 4

1. Choose Set A or Set B of patterned squares.

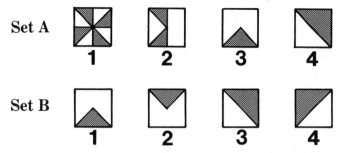

2. Substituting the selected set of patterned squares for the numbers in the latin square, fill in the basic design pattern.

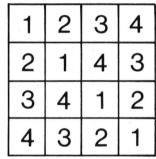

Latin Square

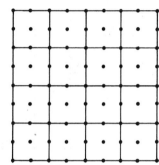

Basic Design Pattern

Are there any lines of symmetry in the latin square? _____

3. Create an 8 x 8 design. Copy your basic design pattern in the upper left corner of the 8 x 8 grid, and complete the design by reflecting the basic pattern over to the other locations.

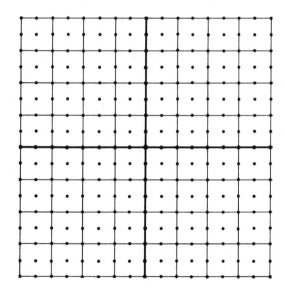

4. Would you get the same 8 x 8 design by using rotations? _____

ACTIVITY: LATIN SQUARE DESIGNS, ORDER 4

1. Assign the numbers 1, 2, 3, and 4 in any order to the patterned squares below.

       ___   ___   ___   ___

2. Construct a latin square of order 4 in which all the elements of the left diagonal are the same.

3. Substituting the patterned squares for the numbers in the latin square, fill in the basic design pattern.

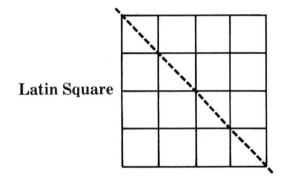

Latin Square

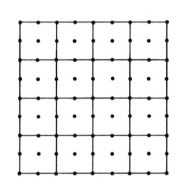

Basic Design Pattern

4. Create an 8 x 8 design. Copy your basic design pattern in the upper left corner of the 8 x 8 grid. Complete the design by using some combination of translations, reflections, or rotations such that the patterned squares of the left diagonal of the finished design *are not* all the same.

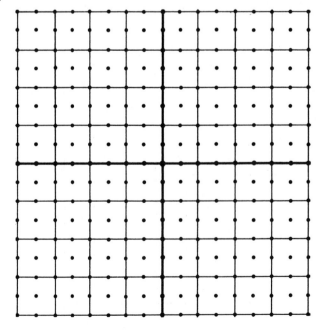

5. What fractional part of your finished design is shaded? ____

58

ACTIVITY: LATIN SQUARE DESIGNS, ORDER 4

1. Color two of these patterned squares with quarter-colorings, and two of them with half-colorings. (Refer to page 19 for instructions on patterned squares.) Assign the numbers 1, 2, 3, and 4 in any order to the patterned squares.

2. Construct a cross latin square of order 4.

3. Substituting the patterned squares for the numbers in the cross latin square, fill in the basic design pattern.

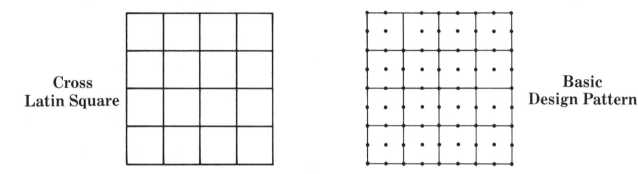

Cross Latin Square

Basic Design Pattern

4. Create an 8 x 8 square design. Copy your basic design pattern in any one of the corners of the 8 x 8 grid. Complete the design by using some combination of translations, reflections, and rotations of the basic pattern to the other locations. Be able to describe how you completed your design.

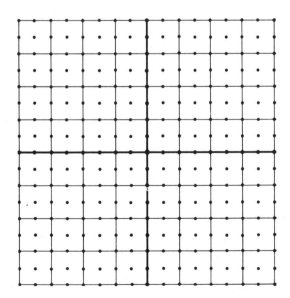

5. What fractional part of your finished design is shaded? _____

ACTIVITY: LATIN SQUARE DESIGNS, ORDER 5

1. Color these patterned squares with quarter-colorings or half-colorings. (Refer to page 19 for instructions on patterned squares.) Assign the numbers 1, 2, 3, 4, and 5 in any order to the patterned squares below.

2. Construct a latin square of order 5.

   Latin Square

3. Substituting the patterned squares for the numbers in the latin square, fill in the basic design pattern.

   Basic Design Pattern

4. On a copy of page A-9, create a 10 x 10 square design. Copy your basic design pattern in any one of the corners of the 10 x 10 grid, and complete the design by using some combination of transformations of the basic pattern to the other locations. Be able to describe how you completed your design.

5. What fractional part of your finished design is shaded? _____

ACTIVITY: LATIN SQUARE DESIGNS, ORDER 6

1. Choose Set A, Set B, or Set C of patterned squares.

Set A   [squares 1–6 with letters x, y, z]

   1   **2**   **3**   **4**   **5**   **6**

   Select three colors: x, y, and z. Color the patterned squares according to the letters marked in them.

Set B   [squares 1–6 with shaded patterns]

   1   **2**   **3**   **4**   **5**   **6**

Set C   [squares 1–6 with dot patterns]

   1   **2**   **3**   **4**   **5**   **6**

   Create your own patterned squares or assign a color to each number.

2. Substituting the selected set of patterned squares for the numbers in the latin square, fill in the basic design pattern.

1	2	3	4	5	6
2	3	1	6	4	5
3	1	2	5	6	4
4	5	6	1	2	3
5	6	4	3	1	2
6	4	5	2	3	1

Latin Square   **Basic Design Pattern**

3. On a copy of page A-9, create a 12 x 12 square design. Copy your basic design pattern in one of the corners of the 12 x 12 grid, and complete the design by reflecting the basic pattern over to the other locations.

4. Would you get the same 12 x 12 design by using rotations? _____

Extensions

On other copies of page A-9, create more designs based on the latin square of order 6 shown above. Use one of the sets of patterned squares above, or create your own set. Use any combination of translations, reflections, and rotations to make a 12 x 12 design.

ACTIVITY: LATIN SQUARE DESIGNS, ORDER 8

1. Choose Set A, Set B, or Set C of patterned squares.

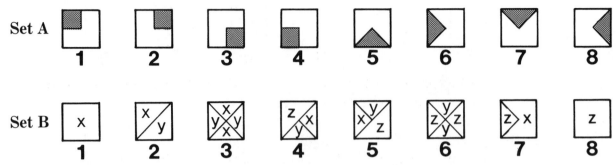

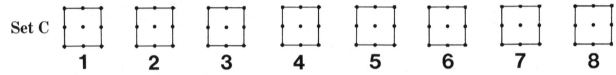

Select three colors: x, y, and z. Color the patterned squares according to the letters marked in them.

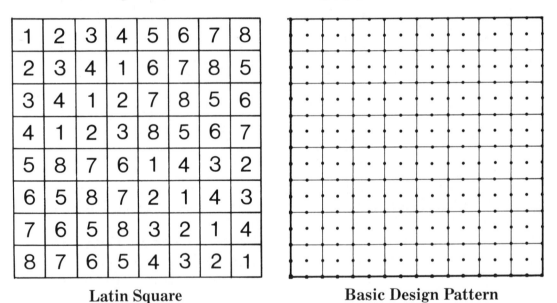

Create your own patterned squares, or assign a color to each number.

2. Substituting the selected set of patterned squares for the numbers in the latin square, fill in the basic design pattern.

1	2	3	4	5	6	7	8
2	3	4	1	6	7	8	5
3	4	1	2	7	8	5	6
4	1	2	3	8	5	6	7
5	8	7	6	1	4	3	2
6	5	8	7	2	1	4	3
7	6	5	8	3	2	1	4
8	7	6	5	4	3	2	1

Latin Square

Basic Design Pattern

3. On a copy of page A-9, create a 16 x 16 square design. Copy your basic design pattern in one of the corners of the 16 x 16 grid, and complete your design by reflecting the basic pattern over to the other locations.

4. Would you get the same design by rotating the basic design pattern? _____

62

ADDITIONAL ACTIVITIES

The grids used for the modular arithmetic tabular designs in Chapter 2 can also be used to create more latin square designs. Use the grids provided on pages A-1 through A-8 of the Appendix, and follow the technique developed in this chapter to create your own latin square designs.

CHAPTER 4

TESSELLATION DESIGNS FROM
PASCAL'S TRIANGLE

A vast variety of designs are possible when the special array of numbers known as *Pascal's triangle* is used in combination with modular arithmetic and geometric grids. In this chapter, we will use modular addition to generate Pascal's triangle patterns on different geometric grids formed from tessellations of geometric shapes, and we will change number into color to create some stunning designs.

PASCAL'S TRIANGLE

Though actually dating back to 1100 A.D. in China and Persia, Pascal's triangle is named for Blaise Pascal (1623–1662), who popularized it in the Western world. This array of numbers is constructed in a triangular shape, with the number 1 repeated along the two sides adjacent to the apex of the triangle; every other number within the triangle equals the sum of the two numbers diagonally above it.

ACTIVITY: PASCAL'S TRIANGLE

Complete the entries in the triangle below.

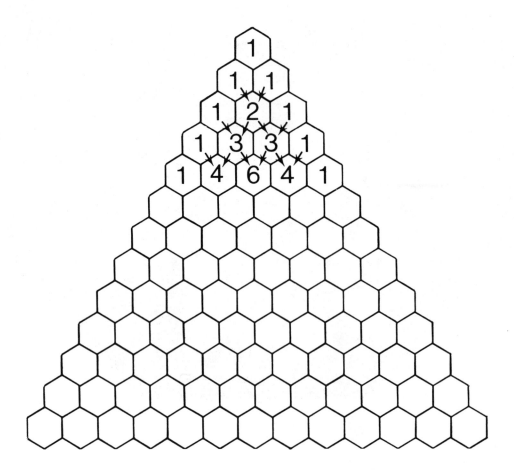

PASCAL'S TRIANGLE AND MODULAR ADDITION

Because each number in the interior of Pascal's triangle is the sum of the two numbers diagonally above it, there are infinitely many different numbers produced by this pattern. Modular addition produces a finite number of different sums and yields a number pattern that can be changed into a design.

Figures 4-1 through 4-4 illustrate how we can create a basic design pattern by using modular addition and Pascal's triangle. We can compute the interior numbers of Pascal's triangle in any modular system we choose, and then substitute colors for the numbers in the triangle.

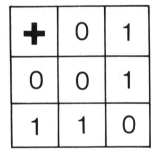

**Figure 4-1
Mod 2 Addition**

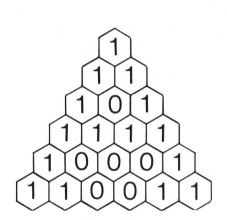

**Figure 4-2
Pascal's Triangle, Mod 2**

**Figure 4-3
Color Code**

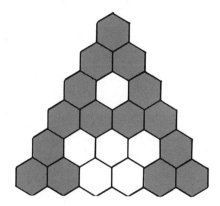

**Figure 4-4
Basic Design Pattern**

Figure 4-1 shows the mod 2 addition table. We fill in the Pascal's triangle by placing the number 1 in each hexagon along the sides adjacent to the apex of the triangle, and filling in the interior numbers using the mod 2 addition table. Then we assign colors to the numbers of the mod 2 table (Figure 4-3), and color each hexagon of the triangle according to the number marked in it. Figure 4-4 shows the basic design pattern that results.

ACTIVITY: PASCAL'S TRIANGLE, MOD 2

1. Complete the Pascal's triangle below, using the mod 2 addition table.

2. Shade in every hexagon marked 1, and leave blank those marked 0.

3. How many small hexagons are there in the entire design? _____ How many small blank hexagons? _____ Small shaded hexagons? _____

+	0	1
0	0	1
1	1	0

Mod 2 Addition

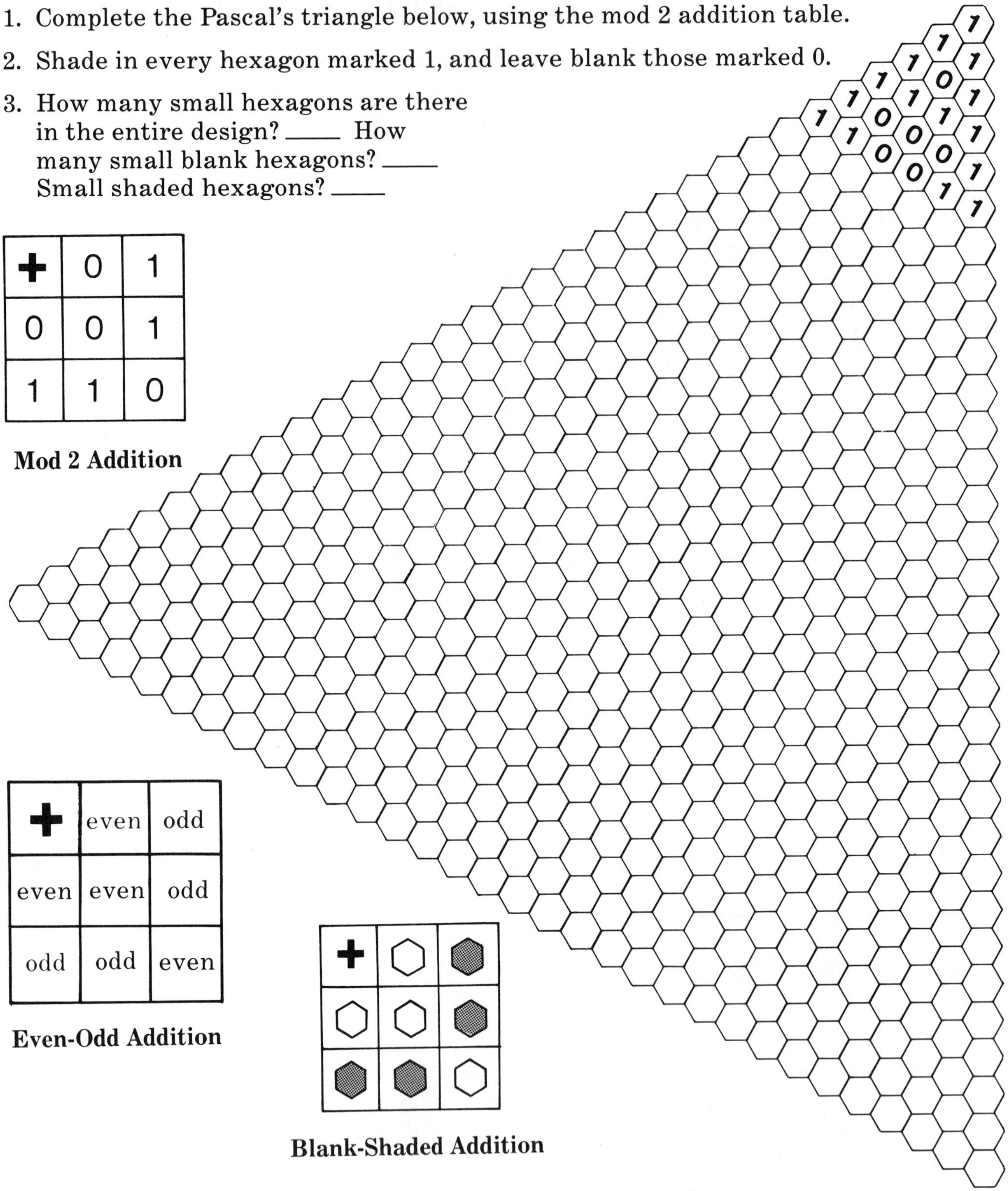

+	even	odd
even	even	odd
odd	odd	even

Even-Odd Addition

+	⬡	⬢
⬡	⬡	⬢
⬢	⬢	⬡

Blank-Shaded Addition

4. Notice the *blank-shaded addition* table and the *even-odd addition* table. The *blank-shaded* table is for the addition of blank and shaded hexagons; the *even-odd* table is for the addition of even and odd numbers. How do they compare with the mod 2 addition table? _____

ACTIVITY: PASCAL'S TRIANGLE, MOD 2

1. Triangular numbers are numbers that produce a triangular pattern of objects as shown below. Name the next 8 triangular numbers.

Use the design on page 68 to complete the following exercises.

2. List in order from smallest to largest the triangular numbers formed by the *blank* hexagons. Then count how many times each triangular number appears in the design.

Triangular Number	How Many?
_____	_____
_____	_____
_____	_____
_____	_____

Is there a pattern that describes how many of each triangular number appear in the design? If so, describe it. _____

3. The rows of Pascal's triangle are numbered as shown in Figure 4-5. The triangle has been shaded according to this shading code: Shade in every hexagon marked 1; leave blank those marked 0.

Figure 4-5

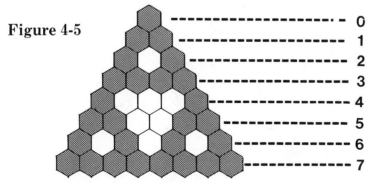

Complete the chart by naming the rows that contain *only shaded hexagons*. Then try to extend the pattern.

Row Number	0	1	3	7											
Number of Shaded Hexagons in Row	1	2													

Describe the row-number pattern: _____
Describe the shaded-hexagon number pattern: _____

ACTIVITY: PASCAL'S TRIANGLE, MOD 2

The Pascal's triangle in Figure 4-6 has been completed in mod 2 addition on a square grid, with the grid placed diagonally. This mod 2 number pattern has been copied in triangle A below, with shaded squares replacing the squares marked 1, and blank squares replacing the squares marked 0. Triangle A will be used as a basic design pattern.

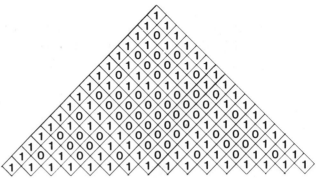

Figure 4-6
Pascal's Triangle, Mod 2

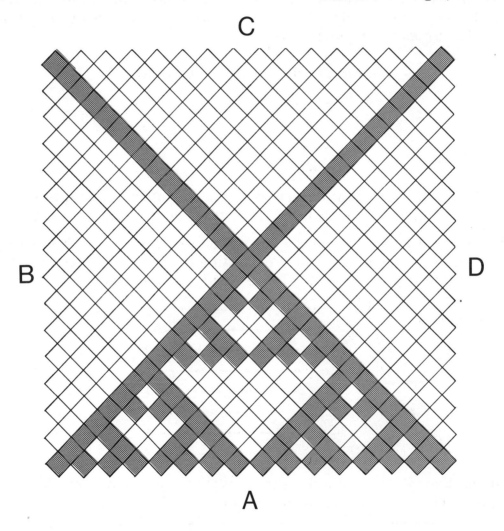

Complete the square design by rotating the basic design pattern to triangles B, C, and D. (The four triangles overlap along the rows of 1's, and this shading has been completed for you.) To see what your finished design should look like, you could look into two small mirrors placed along the sides of triangle A such that the mirrors meet at the center of the square.

ACTIVITY: PASCAL'S TRIANGLE, MOD 2

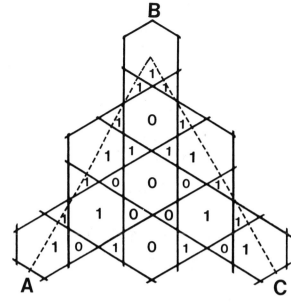

Pascal's triangle designs can be constructed on grids formed by one or more geometric shapes. The mod 2 Pascal's triangle array used in this activity has been placed on a tessellation of regular triangles and hexagons.

1. On triangle ABC shade in one color all of the regions marked 1; leave blank those regions marked 0, or shade them with a second color.

2. Color triangle DEF in the same way as triangle ABC, extending the Pascal's triangle pattern to fill the entire design.

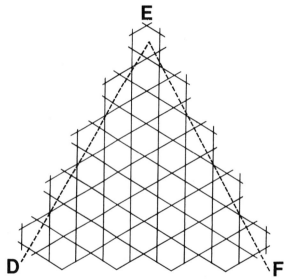

Extension

Six of these triangular grids can be placed together to form a hexagon because the measure of ∠ ABC is 60°, and 6 × 60° = 360°. Figure 4-7 shows the six triangular grids placed together in the tessellation of regular triangles and hexagons. On a copy of page A-10, create a hexagonal design by coloring each of the six triangular grids in the same pattern that you colored triangle DEF. If you wish to see what your finished design should look like, you could look into two mirrors placed along $\overline{DE}$ and $\overline{FE}$, meeting at E.

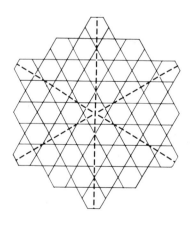

Figure 4-7

71

ACTIVITY: PASCAL'S TRIANGLE, MOD 3

1. Complete the mod 3 addition table.

2. A mod 3 Pascal's triangle array has been started in the tessellation of regular hexagons below. Complete the triangle using mod 3 addition.

3. With your pencil, lightly shade in all the hexagons marked 1 or 2, and leave blank those marked 0.

4. How many small hexagons are there in the entire design? _____ How many small blank hexagons? _____ Small shaded hexagons? _____

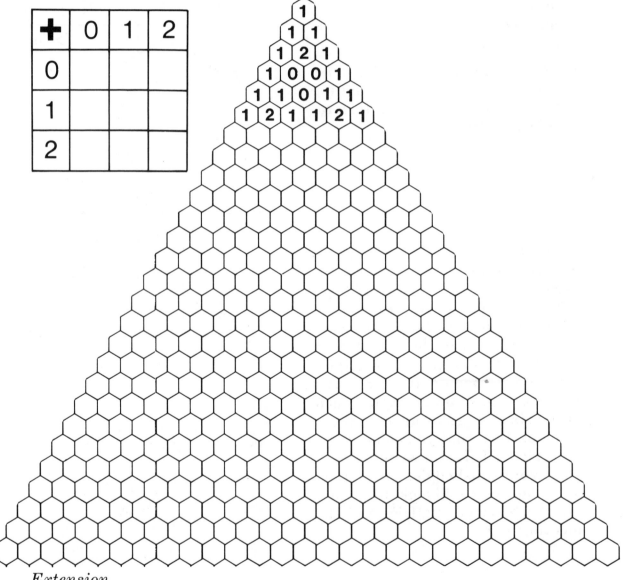

Extension

Six of these triangular grids can be placed together (with the outside edges of the grids overlapping) to make a hexagonal design. On a copy of page A-11, color each of the six triangles, using the coloring pattern above.

ACTIVITY: PASCAL'S TRIANGLE, MOD 3

1. List the first 10 triangular numbers: ————————————

Use the design on page 72 to complete the exercises below.

2. What triangular number is formed by the shaded hexagons? ————
   How many triangles of this kind are formed? ————

3. List in order from smallest to largest the triangular numbers formed
   by the blank hexagons. Then count how many times each triangular
   number appears in the design.

Triangular Number	How Many?
————	————
————	————

   Challenge!

   If the design were extended many more rows, what would be the
   next triangular number formed by blank hexagons? ————

4. Complete the chart naming the rows that contain *only shaded
   hexagons*. (Remember, the top row in Pascal's triangle is row 0.)

Row Number	0	1	2				
Number of Shaded Hexagons in Row	1	2					

The design on page 72 ends at row 26. Study the design carefully and
predict what the next three rows would be:

	Total Hexagons	Blank Hexagons	Shaded Hexagons
Row 27	————	————	————
Row 28	————	————	————
Row 29	————	————	————

Challenge!

Study the chart above which names the rows that contain only
shaded hexagons. Can you predict the next four rows in which only
shaded hexagons will appear? ———— ———— ———— ————

ACTIVITY: PASCAL'S TRIANGLE, MOD 3

1. A mod 3 Pascal's triangle has been placed in triangle ABC, a tessellation of squares, regular hexagons, and nonregular hexagons. Shade in one color all of the regions marked 1; shade in a second color all of the regions marked 2; leave blank the regions marked 0.

2. Color triangle DEF in the same way as triangle ABC, extending the Pascal's triangle pattern to fill the entire design.

Extension

Six of these triangular grids can be placed together to form a hexagon because ∠ABC measures 60°, and 6 × 60° = 360°. Figure 4-8 shows the six triangular grids placed together in a tessellation of squares and hexagons. On a copy of page A-12, create a hexagonal design by coloring each of the six triangular grids in the same pattern that you colored triangle DEF. If you wish to see what your finished design should look like, you could look into two mirrors placed along $\overline{DE}$ and $\overline{FE}$, meeting at E.

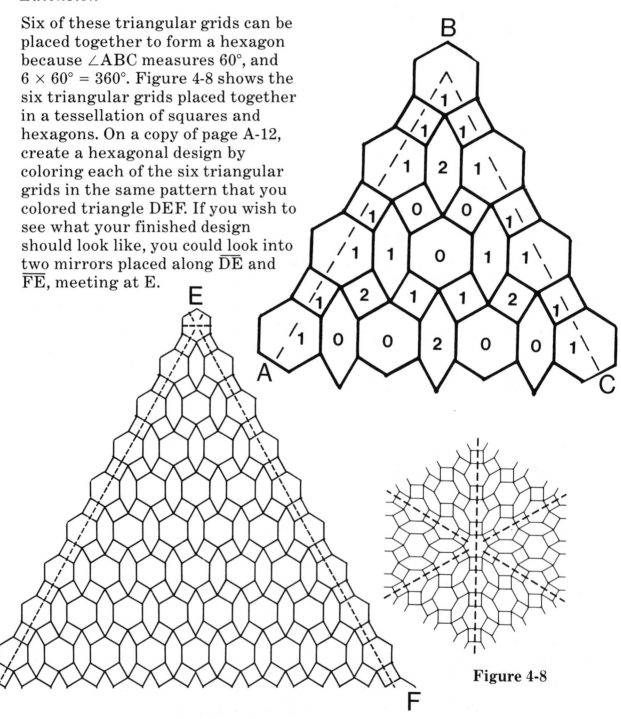

Figure 4-8

74

ACTIVITY: PASCAL'S TRIANGLE, MOD 4

1. Complete the mod 4 addition table.

+	0	1	2	3
0				
1				
2				
3				

2. A mod 4 Pascal's triangle array has been started in the tessellation of regular hexagons below. Complete the triangle using mod 4 addition.

3. With your pencil, lightly shade in all hexagons marked 1, 2, 3, and leave blank those hexagons marked 0.

4. How many small hexagons are there in the entire design? _____ How many small blank hexagons? _____ Small shaded hexagons? _____

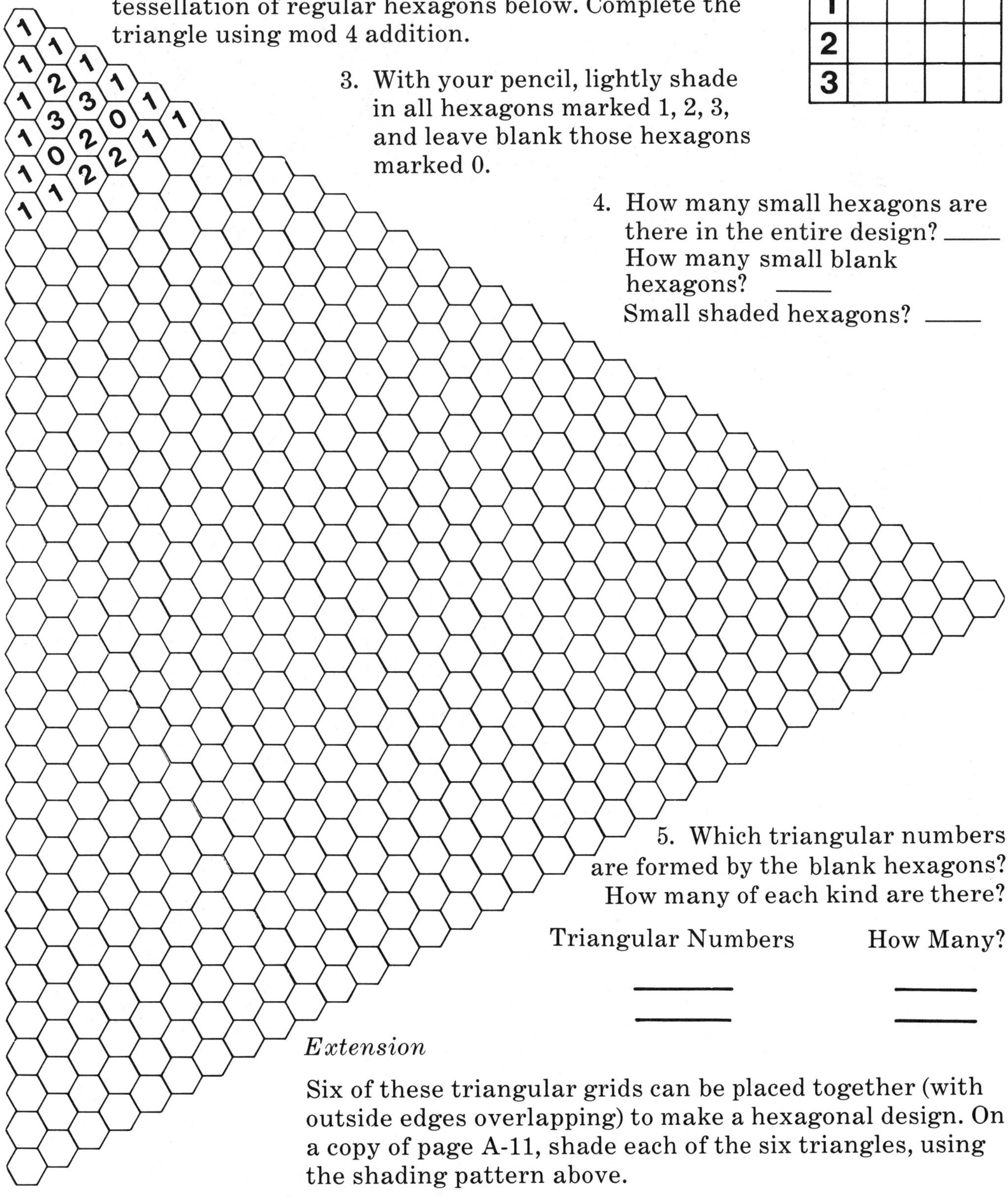

5. Which triangular numbers are formed by the blank hexagons? How many of each kind are there?

Triangular Numbers   How Many?

_____   _____

_____   _____

Extension

Six of these triangular grids can be placed together (with outside edges overlapping) to make a hexagonal design. On a copy of page A-11, shade each of the six triangles, using the shading pattern above.

ACTIVITY: PASCAL'S TRIANGLE, MOD 4

1. Complete the Pascal's triangle arrays in triangles BDC and ADB, using mod 4 addition.

2. Assign a different color to each of the numbers 1, 2, and 3. Color each of the four triangles in the design below, using the colors selected for 1, 2, 3, and leaving blank the regions marked 0. Color triangle ADE in the same pattern as triangle BDC; color triangle CDE in the same pattern as triangle ADB.

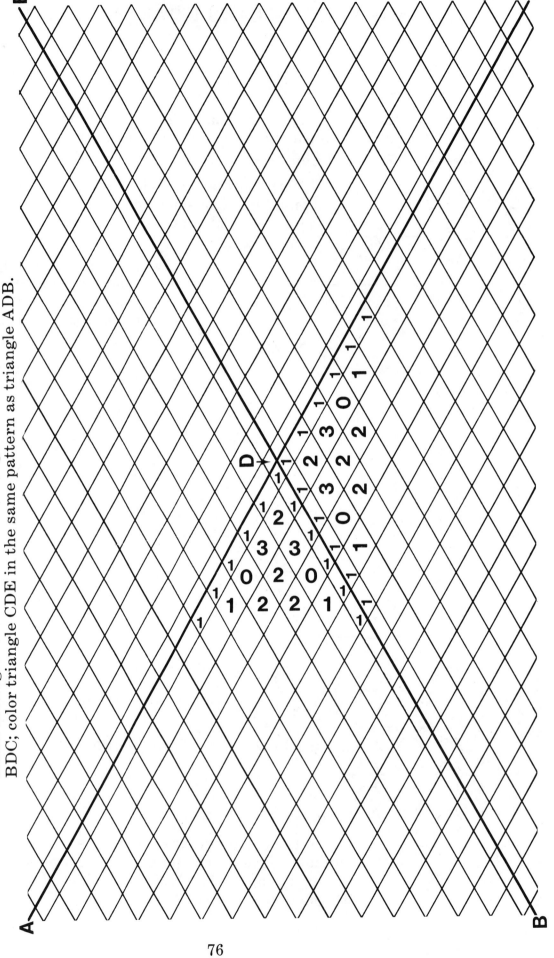

ACTIVITY: PASCAL'S TRIANGLE, MOD 5

1. A mod 5 Pascal's triangle has been started in triangle ABC, a tessellation of 72°–108° rhombi. Complete the triangle using mod 5 addition.

2. Assign a different color to each of the numbers 1, 2, 3, and 4. Color the rhombi according to the numbers marked in them; leave blank the rhombi marked 0.

3. Five of these triangular grids can be placed together to form a pentagon because the measure of ∠ABC is 72° and 5 × 72° = 360°. The figure below shows the triangular grids placed together in a modified tessellation of rhombi. To create a pentagonal design, color each of the five triangles in the same pattern that you colored triangle ABC.

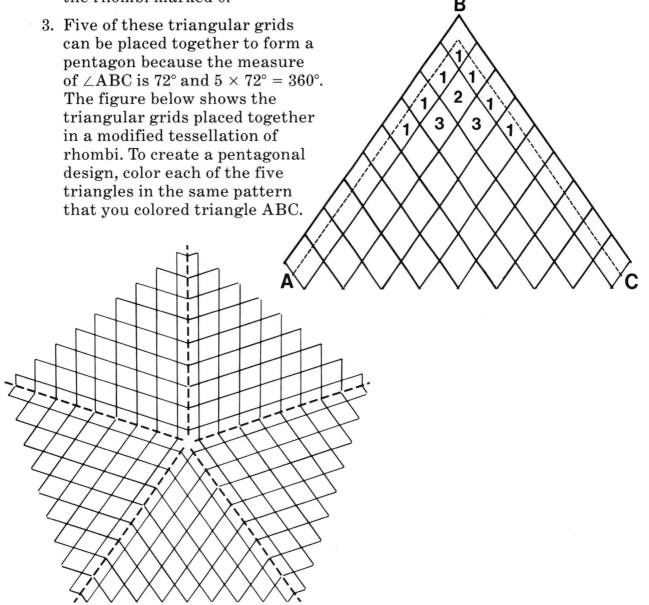

Extension

Extend the pentagonal design to a larger area on a copy of page A-15.

ACTIVITY: PASCAL'S TRIANGLE, MOD 5

1. Triangle ABC shows a mod 5 Pascal's triangle in a tessellation of regular hexagons. Assign a different color to each of the numbers 1, 2, 3, and 4. Color the hexagons in triangle ABC according to the numbers marked in them; leave blank those hexagons marked 0.

2. In triangle ABC, how many hexagons are colored? _____ How many hexagons are blank? _____ Which triangular numbers are formed by blank hexagons? _____

3. Color the six triangles in the hexagonal design below using the same pattern that you used to color triangle ABC.

Extension

Extend the hexagonal design to a larger area on a copy of page A-11.

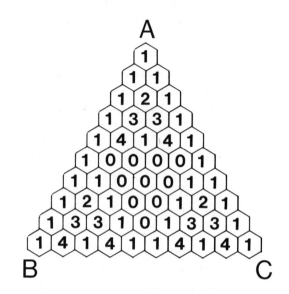

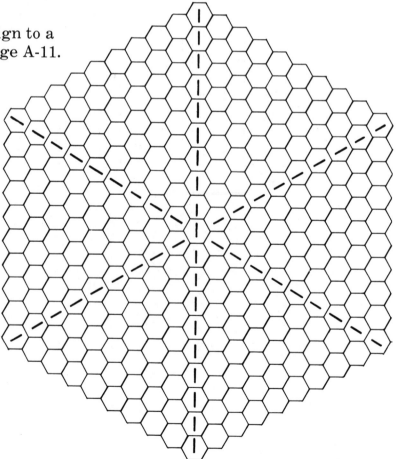

78

ACTIVITY: PASCAL'S TRIANGLE, MOD 6

1. A mod 6 Pascal's triangle has been started in a tessellation of regular hexagons. Complete the triangle using mod 6 addition.

2. Assign a different color to each of the numbers 1, 2, 3, 4, and 5. Color the hexagons according to the numbers marked in them; leave blank those hexagons marked 0.

3. Color the six triangles in the hexagonal design below, using the same pattern that you used to color triangle ABC.

Extension

Extend the hexagonal design to a larger area on a copy of page A-11.

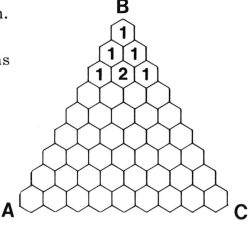

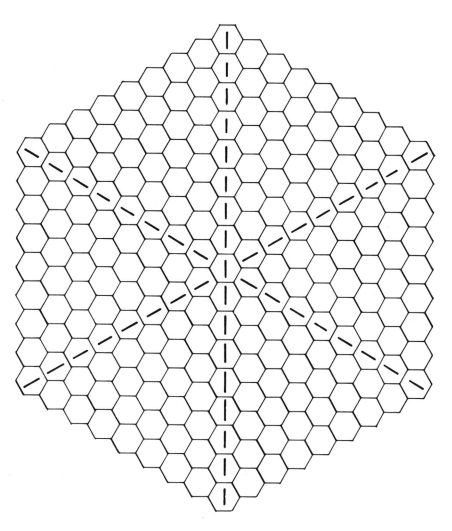

ACTIVITY: PASCAL'S TRIANGLE MOD 6

1. A mod 6 Pascal's triangle has been started in triangle ABC, a tessellation of 45°−135° rhombi. Complete the triangle using mod 6 addition.

2. Assign a different color to each of the numbers 1, 2, 3, 4, and 5. Color the rhombi in triangle ABC according to the numbers marked in them; leave blank those rhombi marked 0.

3. Eight of these triangular grids can be placed together to form an octagon because the measure of ∠ABC is 45° and 8 × 45° = 360°. The figure below shows the triangular grids placed together in a modified tessellation of rhombi. To create an octagonal design, color each of the eight triangles in the same pattern you used to color triangle ABC.

Extension

Extend the octagonal design to a larger area on a copy of page A-16.

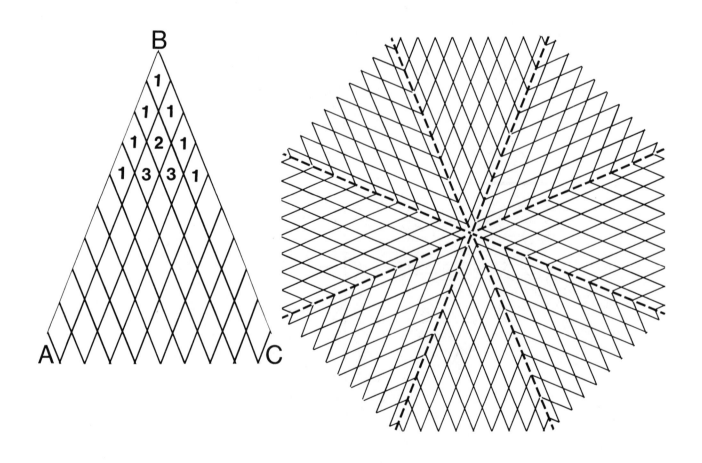

PASCAL'S RIGHT TRIANGLE

We can construct a Pascal's right triangle on square grid paper. We place the number 1 in each square of the left column and in each square along the right diagonal from the top square. We find every other number by adding the number directly above it and the number to the left of the number directly above it.

ACTIVITY: PASCAL'S RIGHT TRIANGLE

1. Complete the Pascal's right triangle below.

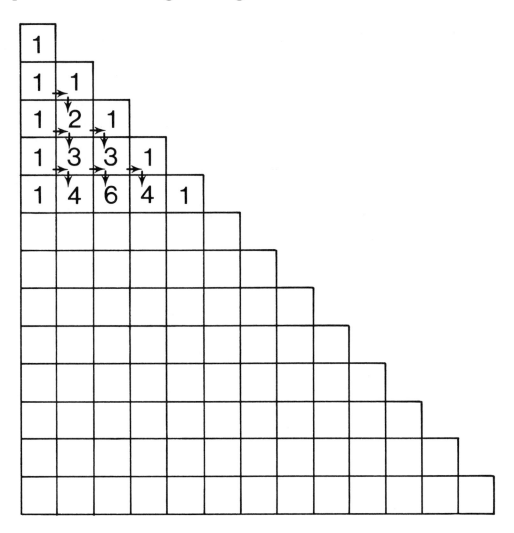

2. Lightly shade in all squares marked with odd numbers.

3. In the right triangle above, which is larger—the number of odd numbers or the number of even numbers? _____

ACTIVITY: PASCAL'S RIGHT TRIANGLE, MOD 2

1. The Pascal's right triangle in Figure 4-9 has been completed in mod 2 addition. A part of this mod 2 pattern has been copied in triangle A below, with shaded squares replacing those marked 1, and blank squares replacing those marked 0. Complete the shading of triangle A.

2. Reflect the shaded pattern onto right triangle B. Notice that triangle A and triangle B overlap along the diagonal of the square design.

3. Reflect the pattern from triangles A and B onto the lower half of the square design.

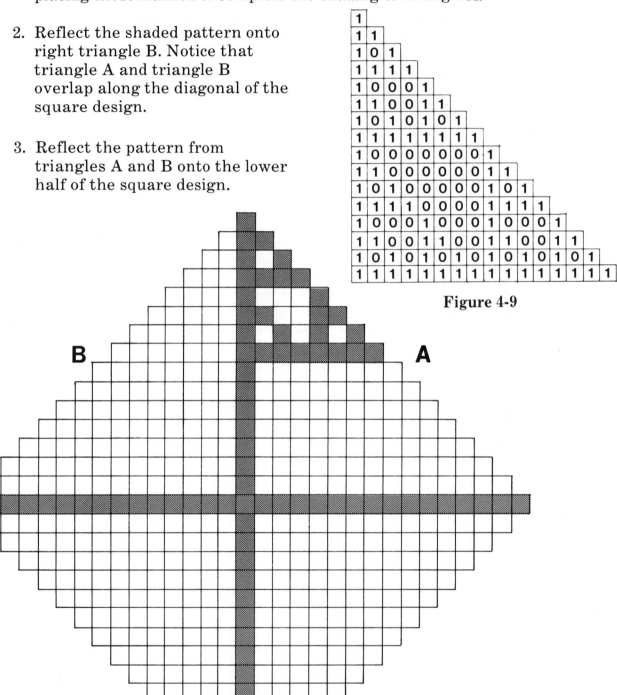

Figure 4-9

82

ADDITIONAL ACTIVITIES

In the preceding activities, we explored only a few of the many designs that can be created by using Pascal's triangle, modular addition, and geometric grids. Pages A-10 through A-19 of the Appendix provide blank grids for you to use for creating your own Pascal's triangle designs. The designs suggested below are ideas to get you started.

Appendix Page	Mod	Shading
A-11	2	Color 1's and 0's different colors.
A-11	3	Color 1's and 2's different colors; leave 0's blank.
A-13 or A-14	3	Color 1's and 2's different colors; leave 0's blank.
A-10	3	Color 1's and 2's different colors; leave 0's blank.
A-15	4	Color 1's, 2's, and 3's different colors; leave 0's blank.
A-15	6	Color 1's, 2's, 3's, 4's, and 5's different colors; leave 0's blank.
A-16	4	Color 1's, 2's, and 3's different colors; leave 0's blank.
A-16	5	Color 1's, 2's, 3's, and 4's different colors; leave 0's blank.
A-16	2	Color 1's and 0's different colors.
A-10	5	Color 0's, 1's, 2's, 3's, and 4's different colors.

CHAPTER 5

CIRCULAR DESIGNS FROM MODULAR ARITHMETIC PATTERNS

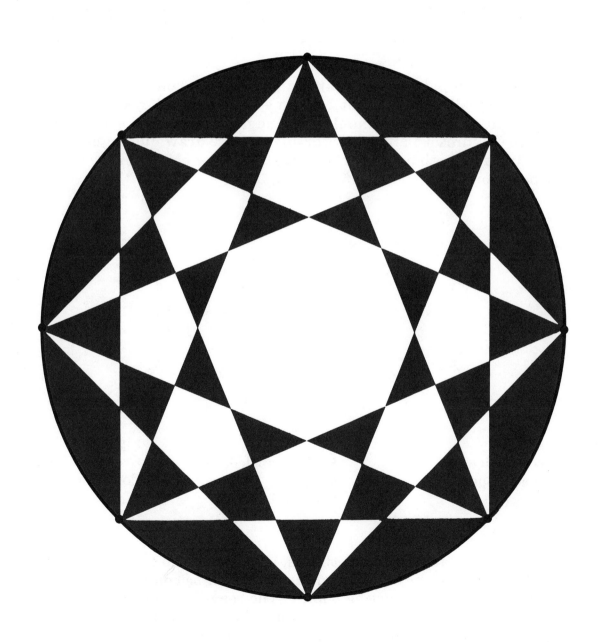

Interesting symmetrical designs can be created if a given number of equally spaced numbered points on a circle are connected according to a pattern that is based on modular arithmetic. In this chapter, we will explore three types of star polygon designs, which are based on modular addition patterns. We will also explore product designs, which are based on modular multiplication patterns.

CIRCULAR DESIGNS FROM MODULAR ADDITION

We generate *star polygons* by connecting every rth point on a circle that has n equally spaced points. Given a circle divided by n equally spaced points, we begin by numbering the points from 0 to n-1, in order clockwise (Figures 5-1 and 5-2). Starting at 0, we draw line segments connecting every rth point on the circle until all n points on the circle have been connected (Figure 5-3).

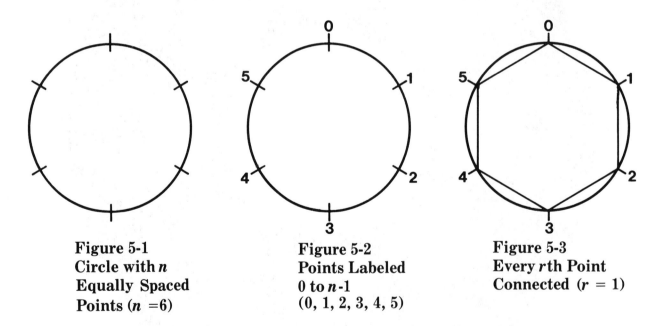

Figure 5-1
Circle with n
Equally Spaced
Points (n =6)

Figure 5-2
Points Labeled
0 to n-1
(0, 1, 2, 3, 4, 5)

Figure 5-3
Every rth Point
Connected (r = 1)

If n and r are relatively prime, that is, if they have no common factors other than 1, all of the n points on the circle will be connected by the time we return to the starting point 0. The resulting design is called a *regular star polygon*. The design shown in Figure 5-3 is a regular star polygon because n (6) and r (1) are relatively prime.

If n and r are *not* relatively prime, that is, if they have common factors other than 1, we return to the starting point 0 before all n points have been connected. This means that we must start again at another point or points to complete the connection of all n points. The resulting design is called a *modified star polygon*. The design shown in Figure 5-4 is a modified star polygon because n (6) and r (2) are not relatively prime.

We can combine two regular star polygons, two modified star polygons, or one of each to form a *double star polygon*. Figure 5-5 shows the double star polygon that results when we combine the Figure 5-3 regular star polygon with the Figure 5-4 modified star polygon.

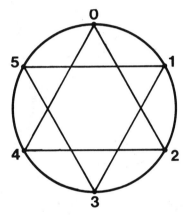

Figure 5-4
Modified Star Polygon
(n = 6 and r = 2)

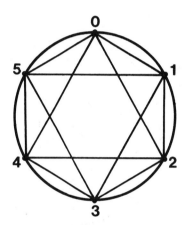

Figure 5-5
Double Star Polygon

Star polygons are represented or described by this notation:

$$\{n \ / \ r\}$$

The circle
is divided
by n equally
spaced points.

Every rth point
is connected.

The notation for the Figure 5-3 star polygon is {6 / 1}; the notation for the Figure 5-4 star polygon is {6 / 2}. The notation for the Figure 5-5 double star polygon is {6 / 1,2}.

Given a circle that has *not* been divided by equally spaced points, we start by locating the n points on the circle. We can locate the points in either of these two ways: (1) Use a protractor to mark off n congruent central angles in the circle, with the measure of each angle equal to 360° divided by n. The line segments which form the congruent angles will also divide the circle into n congruent arcs by n equally spaced points on the circle. (2) Use a protractor to draw one central angle with measure equal to 360° divided by n; find the arc length associated with this angle, and use a compass to mark off this length n times on the circle. Figures 5-6 and 5-7 illustrate these two ways of locating equally spaced points on a circle.

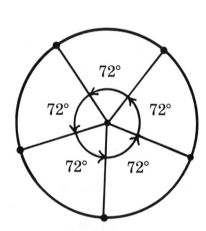

Figure 5-6
Locating n Equally
Spaced Points on
a Circle by Marking
Off Central Angles
$(n = 5)$

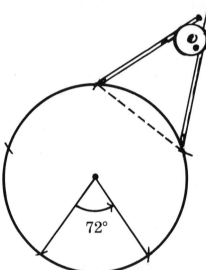

Figure 5-7
Locating n Equally
Spaced Points on
a Circle by Marking
Off Equal Arcs
$(n = 5)$

REGULAR STAR POLYGONS

We illustrate the construction of regular star polygons by two examples. In each of these examples, $n = 5$; hence we begin by locating five equally spaced points on a circle, as shown in Figures 5-6 and 5-7 above. We label the points 0, 1, 2, 3, and 4 in order clockwise. When connecting every rth point, we derive a sequence of numbers which could also be obtained from addition in mod 5. The first example uses $r = 1$; the second, $r = 2$.

Example 1: Draw the regular star polygon {5 / 1}.

Beginning at 0, we connect successive points. The sequence of numbers of the connected points is 0-1-2-3-4-0, which we could also derive by beginning at 0 and adding 1 repeatedly in mod 5 until reaching an answer of 0. Figure 5-8 shows the completed star polygon {5 / 1}, also known as a *regular pentagon*.

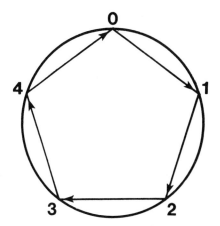

Figure 5-8
Regular Star Polygon {5 / 1}

Example 2: Draw the regular star polygon {5 / 2}.

Beginning at 0, we connect every second point. The sequence of numbers of the connected points is 0-2-4-1-3-0, which we could also derive by starting at 0 and adding 2's repeatedly in mod 5 until reaching an answer of 0. In other words, we could use the mod 5 addition pattern shown below:

0 + 2 = 2, so connect point 0 to point 2;
2 + 2 = 4, so connect point 2 to point 4;
4 + 2 = 1, so connect point 4 to point 1;
1 + 2 = 3, so connect point 1 to point 3
3 + 2 = 0, so connect point 3 to point 0.

The completed star polygon {5 / 2} is shown in Figure 5-9.

Figure 5-9
Regular Star Polygon {5 / 2}

We can now color the constructed star polygon with two colors in such a way that no two adjacent regions within the circle are the same color. The resulting star polygon {5 / 2} design is shown in Figure 5-10.

Figure 5-10
Regular Star Polygon {5 / 2} Design

ACTIVITY: REGULAR STAR POLYGONS

Each of the circles below has five equally spaced points labeled 0, 1, 2, 3, and 4. Draw each star polygon described and write the sequence of numbers that describes how the points are connected.

1. {5 / 1} (Connect successive points.)

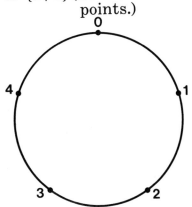

Sequence of numbers: _____

2. {5 / 2} (Connect every second point.)

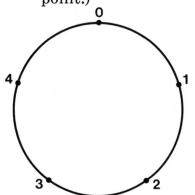

Sequence of numbers:_____

3. {5 / 3} (Connect every third point.)

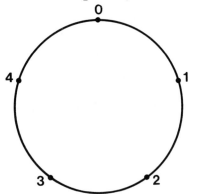

Sequence of numbers: _____

4. {5 / 4} (Connect every fourth point.)

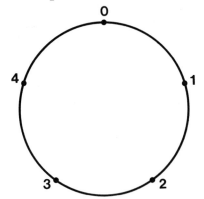

Sequence of numbers:_____

5. {5 / 6} (Connect every sixth point.)

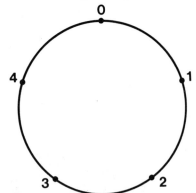

Sequence of numbers: _____

6. {5 / 7} (Connect every seventh point.)

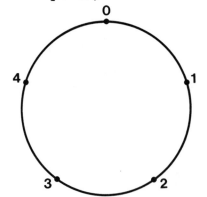

Sequence of numbers: _____

7. How many *different* regular star polygons can be created on a circle divided by five equally spaced points? _____ Can you explain your answer? _____

ACTIVITY: REGULAR STAR POLYGONS

$\{n / r\}$ n and r are relatively prime, and $r<n$.

The circle has n equally spaced points.   Every rth point is connected.

For each value of n, only a finite number of different regular star polygons can be constructed. In this activity, we will explore the number of different regular star polygons that can be constructed if n takes values from 5 to 13. You will need a straightedge, colored pencils, and one or more copies of page A-20 to complete the activity.

1. For each value of n shown in the table below, compute the degree measure of each of the central angles which was used to locate the n equally spaced points on the circle. Record the possible values of r, remembering that r must be less than n, and that n and r must be relatively prime.

2. On the divided circles on page A-20, draw each of the star polygons for the particular values of n and r.

3. Record in the table the number of different regular star polygons that can be constructed for each value of n. The case $n = 5$ has been completed for you, and is illustrated in Figures 5-11 and 5-12.

Number of Equally Spaced Points n	Degree Measure of Each Central Angle $\dfrac{360°}{n}$	Possible Values for r Such That $r<n$ and r and n Are Relatively Prime	Number of Different Star Polygons
5	72°	1,2,3,4	2
6			
7			
8			
9			
10			
11			
12			
13			

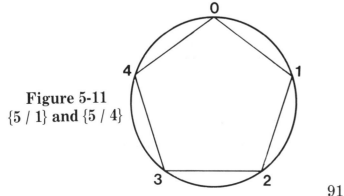

Figure 5-11
$\{5 / 1\}$ and $\{5 / 4\}$

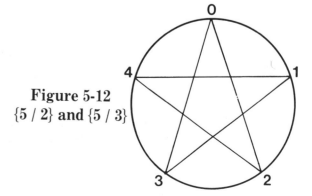

Figure 5-12
$\{5 / 2\}$ and $\{5 / 3\}$

ACTIVITY: REGULAR STAR POLYGONS

Use the information you obtained in the chart on page 91 to complete these exercises.

1. If n is a prime number, find a formula that will give the number of different regular star polygons for n. _____

   _____

2. If n is not a prime number, describe a quick way for finding the number of different regular star polygons for n. _____

   _____

3. In modulo n: $1 + (n-1) = n = 0$

   $2 + (n-2) = n = 0$

   $3 + (n-3) = n = 0$, and so on.

   Such number pairs, whch have a sum of 0, are called *additive inverses*.

   Name the pairs of additive inverses in each modular system below. Note that the numbers in a pair need not be different.

   a. mod 5 (0,0) (1,4) (2,3)_____   b. mod 6 _____

   c. mod 7 _____   d. mod 11 _____

   e. mod 12_____   f. mod 13 _____

4. What conclusion can you make about the regular star polygons for additive inverses $\{n \mid r\}$ and $\{n \mid n-r\}$? _____

   _____

5. On a copy of page A-20, construct the regular star polygons described in the chart below. (Note: In the case of $n = 5$, you may draw your own circles and mark off the points, or you may use the ten-point circle on page A-20 and number the alternate points.) Take $\{n \mid r\}$ with $r>n$ and n,r relatively prime.

n	r	Number of Star Polygons Different From Those on Page 90
5	6, 7, 8, 9	_____
6	7, 11, 13, 17	_____
7	8, 9, 10, 11	_____
8	9, 11, 13, 15	_____

6. What regular star polygons $\{n \mid r\}$ $r>n$ can you name that are different from the regular star polygons $\{n \mid r\}$ $r<n$? _____

92

ACTIVITY: REGULAR STAR POLYGONS

1. Draw these regular star polygons.

2. Color each one using the least number of colors such that no two adjacent regions have the same color.

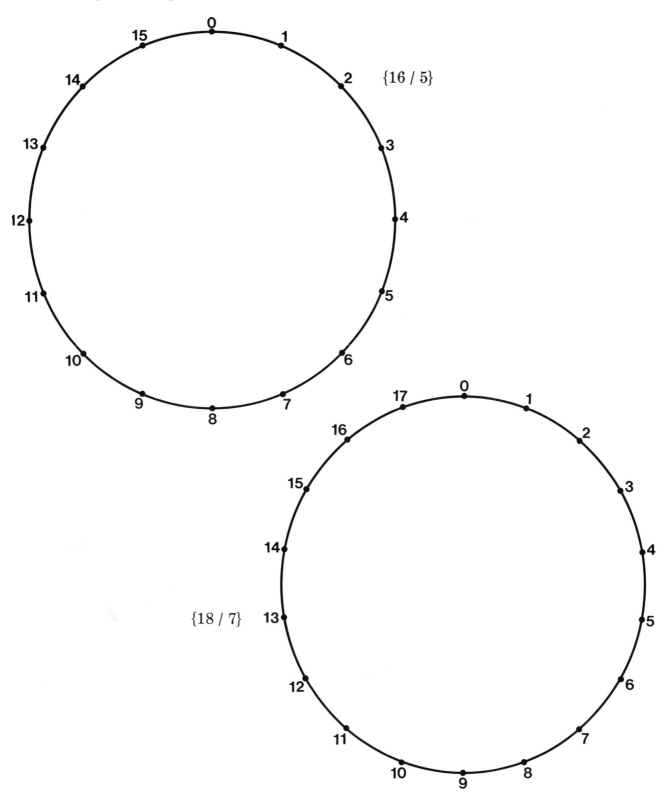

ACTIVITY: REGULAR STAR POLYGONS

1. Draw these regular star polygons.

2. Color each one using the least number of colors such that no two adjacent regions have the same color.

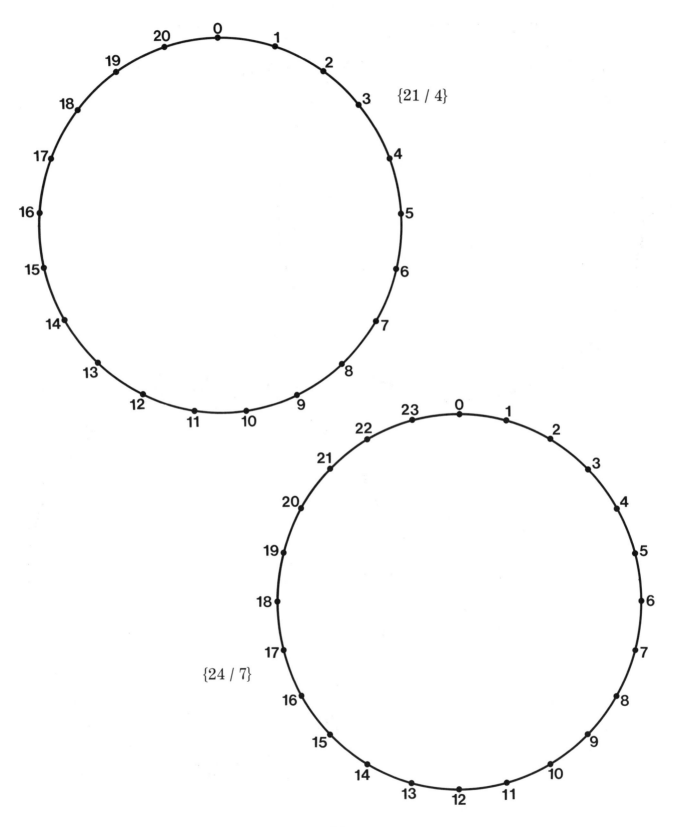

{21 / 4}

{24 / 7}

ACTIVITY: REGULAR STAR POLYGONS

1. On copies of page A-20, draw each of the regular star polygons listed below. (Note: In the cases of $n = 4$ and $n = 5$, you may draw your own circles and mark off the points, or you may use the eight-point and ten-point circles on page A-20, and number alternate points.)

2. Use your protractor to find the approximate degree measure of the inscribed angle at any vertex of the star polygon. Record your results in the chart below.

Example:

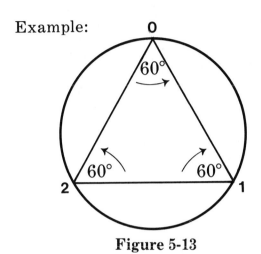

Figure 5-13

Figure 5-13 is the star polygon {3 / 1}. The degree measure of the inscribed angle at any vertex of this star polygon is 60°.

	{n / r}	Degree Measure of Inscribed Angle		{n / r}	Degree Measure of Inscribed Angle
a.	{4 / 1}	_____	b.	{5 / 1}	_____
c.	{5 / 2}	_____	d.	{6 / 1}	_____
e.	{7 / 1}	_____	f.	{7 / 2}	_____
g.	{7 / 3}	_____	h.	{8 / 1}	_____
i.	{8 / 3}	_____	j.	{9 / 1}	_____
k.	{9 / 2}	_____	l.	{10 / 1}	_____
m.	{10 / 3}	_____	n.	{11 / 1}	_____
o.	{n / 1}	_____			

Challenge!

Can you find a formula that gives the degree measure of the inscribed angle at any vertex of a star polygon {n / r}? Verify your formula with the data in the chart above. Hint: Remember that the measure of an inscribed angle is one-half the measure of its intercepted arc.

MODIFIED STAR POLYGONS

In the star polygons that we have considered thus far, n and r have been relatively prime. We will now consider the designs produced when n and r are *not* relatively prime, that is, when n and r have common factors other than 1. We will continue to use the notation $\{n / r\}$ to represent these modified star polygons.

Example 1: Draw the modified star polygon $\{6 / 2\}$ ($n = 6$ and $r = 2$).

We begin by drawing a circle with six equally spaced points, and labeling the points 0, 1, 2, 3, 4, and 5 in a clockwise order. Starting at 0, we connect every second point in the sequence 0-2-4-0, as shown in Figure 5-14. We return to the starting point 0 without touching all six points. We then select a point that has not been touched, say 1. Starting at 1, we connect every second point in the sequence 1-3-5-1, as shown in Figure 5-15. Each of the points has now been touched, as shown in the complete modified star polygon in Figure 5-16.

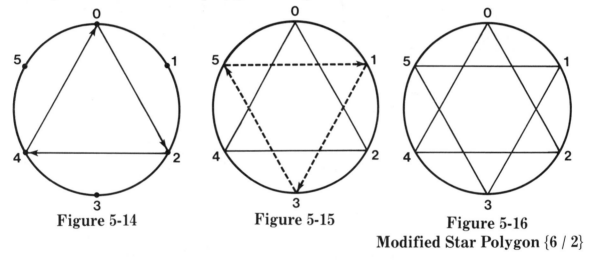

Figure 5-14   Figure 5-15   Figure 5-16

Modified Star Polygon $\{6 / 2\}$

Example 2: Draw the modified star polygon $\{6 / 3\}$ ($n = 6$ and $r = 3$).

Again, we use a circle with six equally spaced points, but this time we connect every third point. Starting at 0, we connect the points in the sequence 0-3-0. Starting again at 1, we join the points in the sequence 1-4-1. Starting again at 2, we join the points in the sequence 2-5-2. The complete modified star polygon is shown in Figure 5-17.

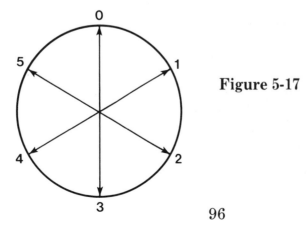

Figure 5-17

96

ACTIVITY: MODIFIED STAR POLYGONS

The circle has n $\{n \, / \, r\}$ Every rth point equally spaced points. ⟋   ⟍ is connected.

n and r are not relatively prime, and $r < n$.

For each value of n, only a finite number of different modified star polygons can be constructed. In this activity, we will explore the number of different modified star polygons that can be constructed for certain values of n. A pattern will emerge, and we will attempt to extend that pattern to a larger value of n. You will need a straightedge, colored pencils, and one or more copies of page A-20 to complete this activity.

1. For each value of n shown in the table below, record the possible values of r, remembering that r must be less than n, and r and n must share a common factor other than 1.

2. On the divided circles on page A-20, draw each of the modified star polygons for the particular values of n and r.

3. Record in the table the number of different modified star polygons that can be constructed for each value of n. The case $n = 6$ has been completed for you, and is illustrated in Figures 5-18 and 5-19.

4. Predict the number of different star polygons for $n = 25$.

Number of Equally Spaced Points n	Possible Values for r Such That $r < n$ and r and n Are Not Relatively Prime	Number of Different Modified Star Polygons
6	**2,3,4**	**2**
8		
9		
10		
12		
〜〜〜	〜〜〜	〜〜〜
25		

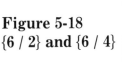

Figure 5-18
$\{6 \, / \, 2\}$ and $\{6 \, / \, 4\}$

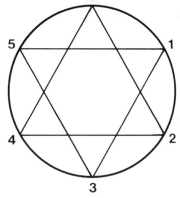

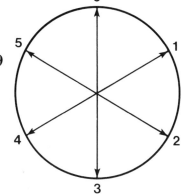

Figure 5-19
$\{6 \, / \, 3\}$

DOUBLE STAR POLYGONS

When two regular star polygons, two modified star polygons, or one of each kind are displayed together in a circular region, the result is called a *double star polygon*. Double star polygons yield fascinating designs. The notation $\{n / r, s\}$ $r, s < n$ is used to represent double star polygons.

Example: Draw the double star polygon $\{5 / 1, 2\}$ ($n = 5$, $r = 1$, $s = 2$).

We begin by drawing star polygon $\{5 / 1\}$ (Figure 5-20). On the same circle, we draw star polygon $\{5 / 2\}$, which by itself is Figure 5-21. The result is Figure 5-22, which is actually Figure 5-20 superimposed on Figure 5-21.

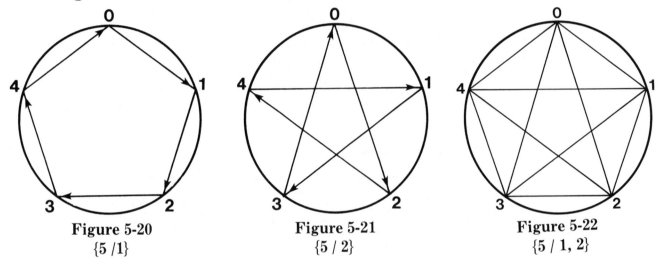

Figure 5-20	Figure 5-21	Figure 5-22
$\{5 / 1\}$	$\{5 / 2\}$	$\{5 / 1, 2\}$

The double star polygon $\{5 / 1, 2\}$ can be colored, now, with the minimum of different colors such that no two adjacent regions have the same color. The resulting double star polygon $\{5 / 1, 2\}$ design is shown in Figure 5-23.

Figure 5-23
Double Star Polygon $\{5 / 1, 2\}$ Design

ACTIVITY: DOUBLE STAR POLYGONS

1. Draw each double star polygon described below.

2. Color each design using the least number of colors such that no two adjacent regions have the same color. Record the minimum number of colors needed to do this.

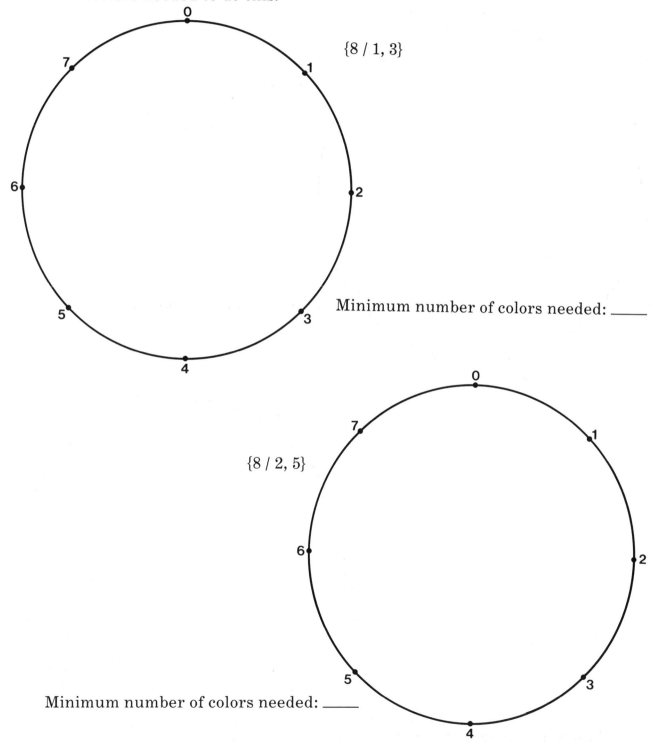

{8 / 1, 3}

Minimum number of colors needed: _____

{8 / 2, 5}

Minimum number of colors needed: _____

ACTIVITY: DOUBLE STAR POLYGONS

1. Draw each double star polygon described below.

2. Color each design using the least number of colors such that no two adjacent regions have the same color. Record the minimum number of colors needed to do this.

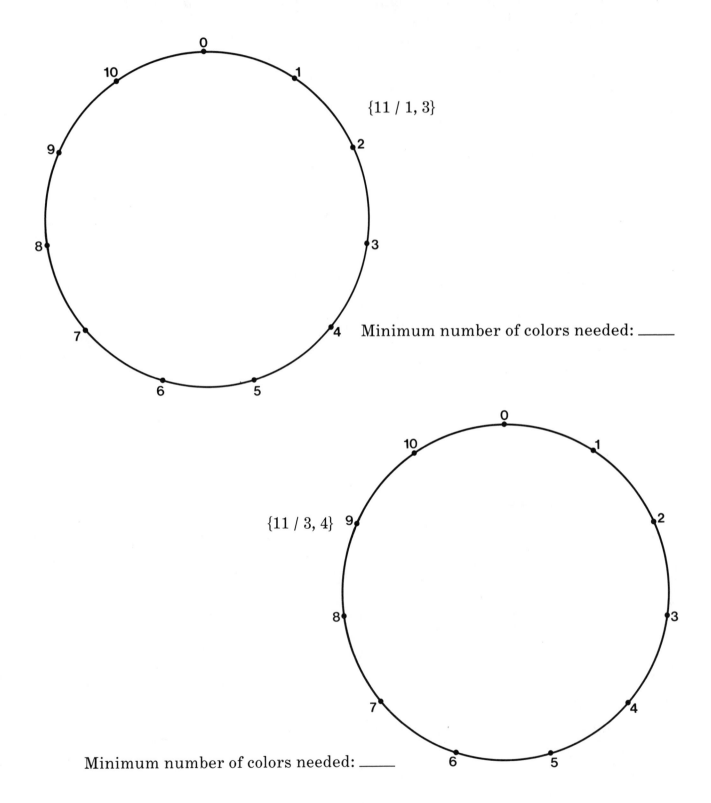

{11 / 1, 3}

Minimum number of colors needed: _____

{11 / 3, 4}

Minimum number of colors needed: _____

ACTIVITY: DOUBLE STAR POLYGONS

1. Draw each double star polygon described below.

2. Color each design using the least number of colors such that no two adjacent regions have the same color. Record the minimum number of colors needed to do this.

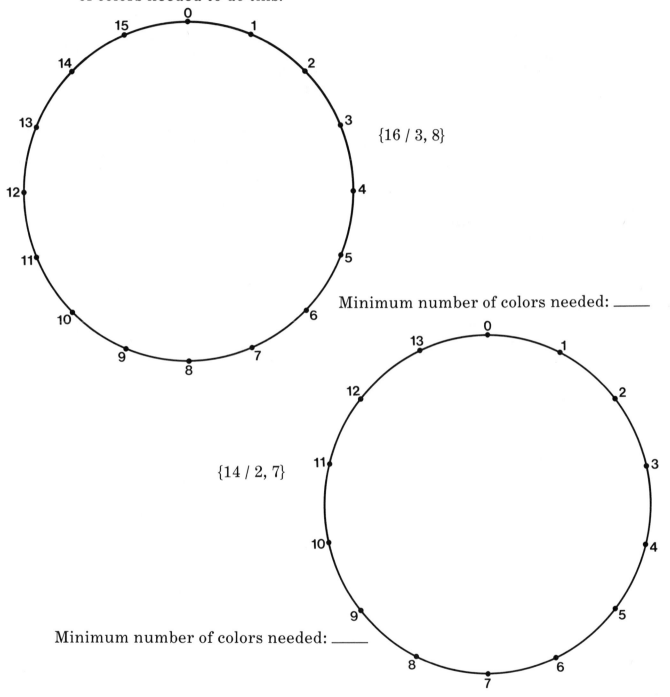

{16 / 3, 8}

Minimum number of colors needed: _____

{14 / 2, 7}

Minimum number of colors needed: _____

Challenge for computer experts!

If your computer has an attached plotter, write a program so that the computer will design star polygons and double star polygons for larger values of n.

CIRCULAR DESIGNS FROM MODULAR MULTIPLICATION

Attractive designs result when equally spaced numbered points on a circle are connected in a sequence based on a modular multiplication pattern. These designs are called *product designs*.

We begin a product design by generating a sequence of numbers which becomes the pattern for connecting the points on the circle. We choose a particular modulo m, and a positive integer p with p between 1 and m. We take p as the first number in the sequence, and generate successive numbers by multiplying repeatedly by p, using mod m multiplication. We end the sequence when we reach p, the starting point. The following examples illustrate how to generate the sequence of numbers and construct the product design from the multiplication pattern.

Example 1: Generate a sequence of numbers with $m = 7$ and $p = 3$. Construct a product design based on this number sequence.

We start with 3, the first number in the sequence. We find successive numbers by multiplying repeatedly by 3, using mod 7 multiplication. (To multiply in mod 7, we can use a mod 7 multiplication table or we can use this algorithm: Multiply in the ordinary way and divide the product by 7; the remainder will be the product in mod 7.) Using this algorithm, we generate the following sequence:

$$p = 3$$
$$3 \times 3 = 9 = 2 \ (\text{mod } 7)$$
$$3 \times 2 = 6 = 6 \ (\text{mod } 7)$$
$$3 \times 6 = 18 = 4 \ (\text{mod } 7)$$
$$3 \times 4 = 12 = 5 \ (\text{mod } 7)$$
$$3 \times 5 = 15 = 1 \ (\text{mod } 7)$$
$$3 \times 1 = 3 = 3 \ (\text{mod } 7)$$

The sequence we generate with $m = 7$ and $p = 3$ is 3, 2, 6, 4, 5, 1, 3.

The numbers in this sequence include every natural number from 1 to $m-1$ (that is, from 1 to 6).

To construct a design based on this sequence, we use a circle with $m-1$ (6) equally spaced points, and label the points from 1 to $m-1$ (1 to 6) as shown in Figure 5-24. We draw straight line segments connecting the points in the sequence 3-2-6-4-5-1-3, which results in the product design shown in Figure 5-25. Can you find one line of symmetry in this product design?

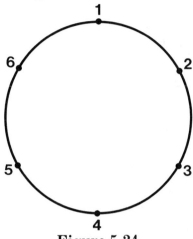

Figure 5-24
Points Labeled 1 to m-1

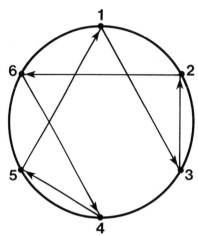

Figure 5-25
Product Design [7 / 3]

Product designs are represented or described by this notation:

$$[m \, / \, p]$$

Modulo $\nearrow$ $\nwarrow$ Constant multiplier

In example 2, the sequence of numbers generated by starting with p does *not* include all the natural numbers from 1 to $m-1$. In this case, it is necessary for us to choose an additional starting number and to generate a second sequence.

Example 2: Construct the product design [7 / 2].

Starting with $p = 2$, we generate a sequence by multiplying repeatedly by 2, using mod 7 multiplication. Using the algorithm explained in example 1, we generate the following sequence:

$$p = 2$$
$$2 \times 2 = 4 = 4 \,(\text{mod } 7)$$
$$2 \times 4 = 8 = 1 \,(\text{mod } 7)$$
$$2 \times 1 = 2 = 2 \,(\text{mod } 7)$$

The sequence we generate with $m = 7$ and $p = 2$ is 2, 4, 1, 2.

103

Since the sequence of products 2, 4, 1, 2 reaches the starting number 2 without including all the natural numbers from 1 to 6, we select one of the unused numbers, say 3, and use it as the starting number for another sequence. Again multiplying repeatedly by 2, we generate the second sequence:

$$3 \text{ (Starting number)}$$

$2 \times 3 =$	$6 =$	$6 \pmod 7$
$2 \times 6 =$	$12 =$	$5 \pmod 7$
$2 \times 5 =$	$10 =$	$3 \pmod 7$

The sequence we generate with $m = 7$ and $p = 2$, starting with 3, is 3, 6, 5, 3.

This sequence 3, 6, 5, 3, when combined with the first sequence 2, 4, 1, 2, includes all the natural numbers from 1 to 6.

To construct a design based on these two sequences of numbers, we use a circle with $m-1$ (6) equally spaced points, labeled from 1 to $m-1$ (1 to 6). We draw straight line segments connecting the points in the sequence 2-4-1-2, then in the sequence 3-6-5-3. The product design that results is shown in Figure 5-26.

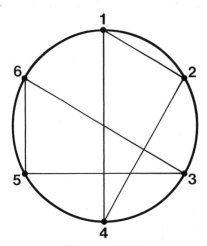

Figure 5-26
Product Design [7 / 2]

Can you find one line of symmetry in this product design?

ACTIVITY: PRODUCT DESIGNS

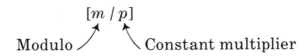

$$[m \mid p]$$

Modulo ⟋ ⟍ Constant multiplier

1. Draw the product designs [7 / 4], [7 / 5], and [7 / 6].

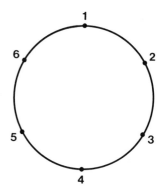

2. Draw the product designs [9 / 2], [9 / 4], [9 / 5], and [9 / 7].

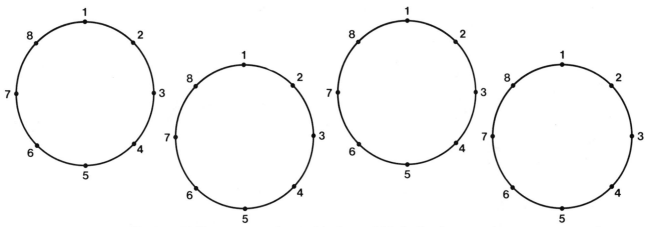

3. Draw all the *different* product designs [11 / p] where p is any natural number such that 1<p<11.

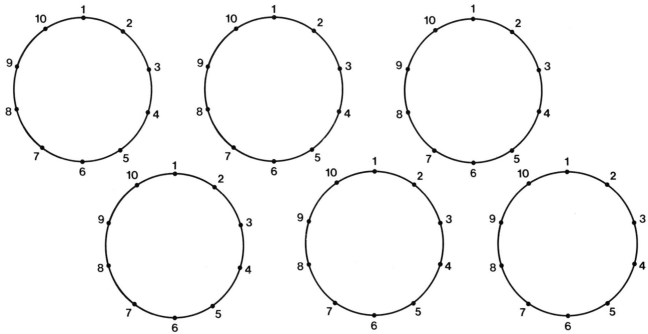

105

4. Draw all the different product designs [13 / p] where p is any natural number such that 1<p<13.

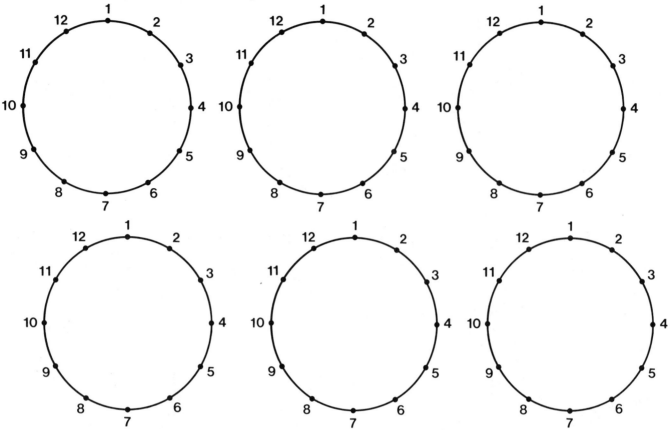

5. In mod 5, 1 × 1 = 1, 2 × 3 = 1, and 4 × 4 = 1. Such number pairs, which have a product of 1, are called *multiplicative inverses*. Note that the numbers in a pair need not be different. Can 0 be in a number pair of multiplicative inverses? _____

   Name the pairs of multiplicative inverses in each modular system below.

   a. mod 7 <u>(1,1) (2,4) (3,5) (6,6)</u>   b. mod 11 _____
   c. mod 13 _____   d. mod 8   _____
   e. mod 9 _____   f. mod 12 _____

6. Study exercises 1 through 5. Complete the following statement. The product designs [m / a] and [m / b] where a × b = 1 in mod m are _____

7. Look at the product designs drawn in exercises 1 through 4. How many lines of symmetry are in each of the product designs?

   a. [11 / 2] __1 line__ b. [11 / 3] _____ c. [11 / 5] _____
   d. [11 / 7] _____   e. [11 / 10] _____ f. [13 / 2] _____
   g. [13 / 3] _____   h. [13 / 4] _____   i. [13 / 5] _____
   j. [13 / 6] _____   k. [13 / 9] _____   l. [13 / 12] _____

ACTIVITY: PRODUCT DESIGNS

1. Draw the product designs described below.

2. Color the regions using the least number of colors such that no two adjacent regions have the same color.

3. Record how many lines of symmetry there are in each design.

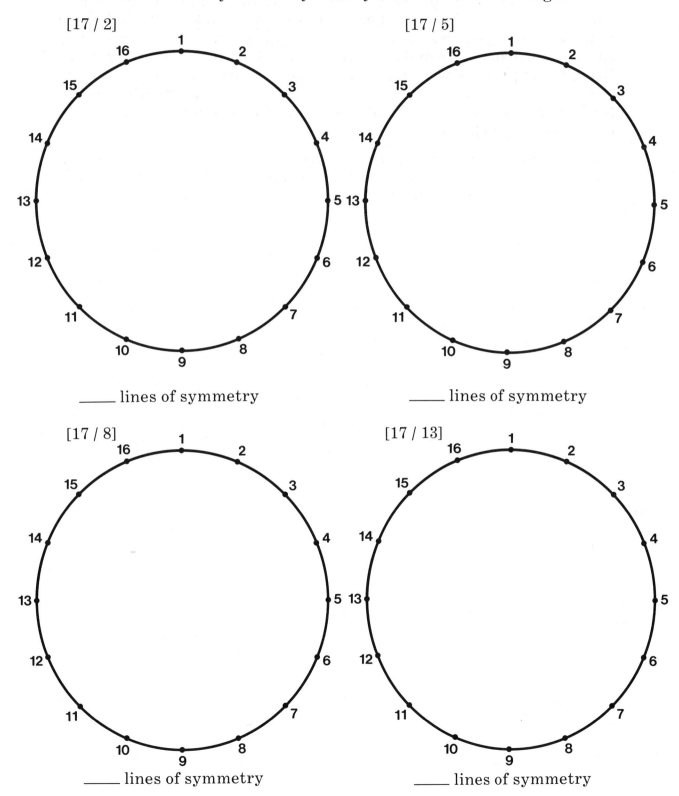

[17 / 2]

_____ lines of symmetry

[17 / 5]

_____ lines of symmetry

[17 / 8]

_____ lines of symmetry

[17 / 13]

_____ lines of symmetry

ADDITIONAL ACTIVITIES

Star polygons and product designs make terrific string art creations for larger values of n. On a large sheet of paper, draw a circle and mark the desired number of equally spaced points on it. (You might begin with 32 points or 64 points. Because these numbers are powers of 2, circles can easily be subdivided into 32 or 64 points.) Tape the divided circle onto a sheet of wood and drive nails into the wood at each of the division marks. Remove the paper pattern from the board. Tie a piece of colored string, thread, or yarn to one of the nails which will act as your starting point. Now, instead of drawing segments, use the string to connect the points in the pattern you choose.

You may wish to make more than one design on your board. If so, try using a different color of string for each of the designs you make, and begin each design at a different height on the nails.

CHAPTER 6

LINE DESIGNS FROM MAGIC SQUARES

MAGIC SQUARES

A *magic square* is a square table of numbers such that: (1) the total number of elements in the table equals n^2; (2) each row and column contains n elements; and (3) *the sum of the elements in every row, column, and diagonal are equal.* The sum is called the *magic constant.* Figure 6-1 shows a magic square that has a magic constant of 15.

A magic square in an n x n array is called an *nth order magic square.* An nth order magic square in which the positive integers $1, 2, 3, \ldots, n^2$ are used is called a *normal nth order magic square.* The magic square in Figure 6-1 is a normal third order magic square.

Figure 6-1
Normal Third Order Magic Square

MAGIC SQUARE DESIGNS

In our previous work with tabular patterns, we took the square grid, perhaps distorting it first, and replaced the entries of the table with colors and/or patterned squares. The magic square pattern lends itself to a different technique for the construction of designs. Instead of beginning with a grid of squares containing the numbers of the magic square, we will begin with a square array of dots in which each dot is assigned to the corresponding number of the magic square. By connecting the numbered dots in order, we will create a design from the magic square pattern. Figures 6-1 through 6-5 illustrate the procedure that we can use to create a basic design pattern from a normal third order magic square.

•4 •9 •2

•3 •5 •7

•8 •1 •6

Figure 6-2
Magic Square Dot Array

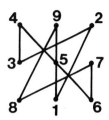

Figure 6-3
Magic Square Line Pattern

Figure 6-4
Magic Square Shaded Pattern

Figure 6-5
Basic Design Pattern

Figure 6–1 shows the third order magic square. We replace the 3 × 3 square grid by a 3 × 3 array of dots, as shown in Figure 6–2. Each of the dots corresponds to an entry in the third order magic square and we so label the points. Then we connect the numbered dots consecutively by line segments; that is, we connect dot 1 to dot 2, dot 2 to dot 3, and so on. As a last step, we connect dot 9 to dot 1—the last dot in the sequence to the first dot. Figure 6–3 shows the finished magic square line pattern.

We now shade the closed regions of the magic square line pattern in such a way that no two adjacent regions are shaded (Figure 6-4). As a last step, we frame the shaded pattern with straight line segments to create the basic design pattern (Figure 6-5).

ACTIVITY: BASIC MAGIC SQUARE DESIGN PATTERNS

1. Check to see that each number array below is a magic square. Write the magic constant in the blank next to the magic square.

2. Label the dot array and draw the line pattern.

3. Copy this line pattern and shade in the closed regions in such a way that no two adjacent regions are shaded. Frame the pattern with line segments to make the basic design pattern.

Line Pattern   **Basic Design Pattern**

4	3	8
9	5	1
2	7	6

_____ Magic constant

2	7	6
9	5	1
4	3	8

_____ Magic constant

4	15	14	1
9	6	7	12
5	10	11	8
16	3	2	13

_____ Magic constant

10	3	15	6
5	16	4	9
8	13	1	12
11	2	14	7

_____ Magic constant

17	24	1	8	15
23	5	7	14	16
4	6	13	20	22
10	12	19	21	3
11	18	25	2	9

_____ Magic constant

112

We can create striking designs by reflecting, translating, or rotating a basic magic square design pattern. For example, Figures 6-6 through 6-8 show the procedure that we can use to extend the magic square pattern to a larger array.

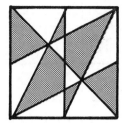

Figure 6-6

Figure 6-6 shows the magic square and corresponding basic design pattern from Figure 6-5. First we copy the basic design pattern in location 1 (Figure 6-7), and then reflect it to locations 2, 3, and 4. This produces the 4 x 4 design in Figure 6-8.

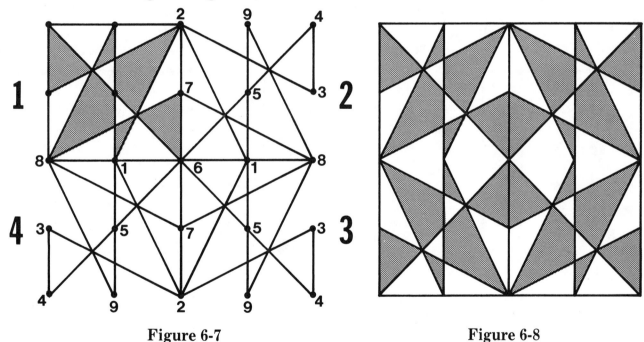

Figure 6-7   **Figure 6-8**

When extending a magic square pattern to a larger array, it is helpful to number the dots in locations 2, 3, and 4, and to draw the three line patterns as guidelines *before* shading the regions.

Do you think that the completed design would have looked the same if the magic square pattern in location 1 had been rotated to locations 2, 3, and 4?

ACTIVITY: MAGIC SQUARE PATTERNS

1. Draw the basic design pattern for the magic square below.

16	3	2	13
5	10	11	8
9	6	7	12
4	15	14	1

Magic Square

Basic Design Pattern

2. Copy your basic design pattern in location 1(a) and location 1(b).
   a. Reflect the basic pattern onto locations 2, 3, and 4 in array (a).
   b. Rotate the basic pattern to locations 2, 3, and 4 in array (b).

a.   **b.**

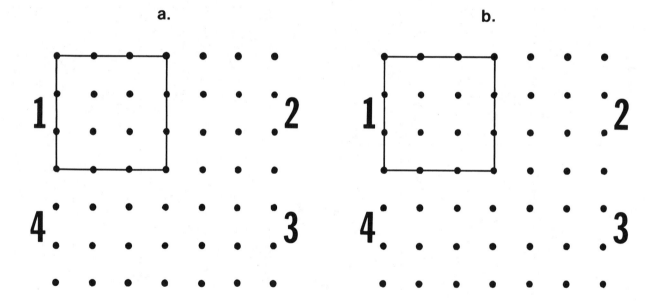

Extension

On a copy of page A-21, try making another basic design pattern using the magic square above. This time, use three different colors instead of black and white. Color the basic design pattern so that no two adjacent regions have the same color. Then use this pattern in location 1 and apply some combination of translations, reflections, or rotations to make the magic square design.

ACTIVITY: MAGIC SQUARE PATTERNS

1. Draw the basic magic square pattern for the magic square below.

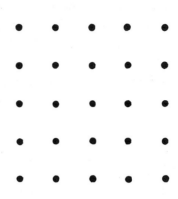

15	8	1	24	17
16	14	7	5	23
22	20	13	6	4
3	21	19	12	10
9	2	25	18	11

Magic Square   **Basic Design Pattern**

2. Copy your basic design pattern in location 1 (a) and location 1 (b).
   a. Reflect the basic pattern onto locations 2, 3, and 4 in array (a).
   b. Rotate the basic pattern to locations 2, 3, and 4 in array (b).

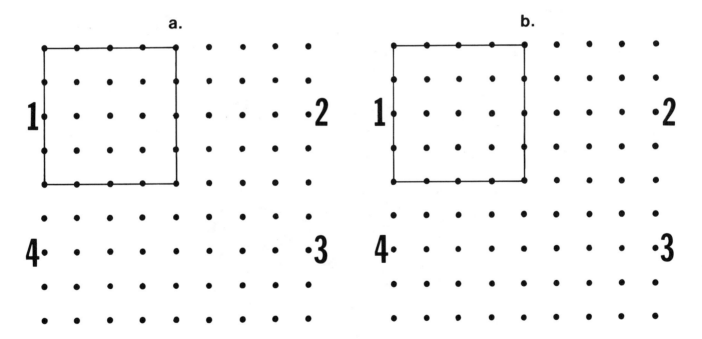

Extension

On a copy of page A-21, try making another basic design pattern using the magic square above. This time, use three different colors instead of black and white. Color the basic design pattern so that no two adjacent regions have the same color. Then use this pattern in location 1 and apply some combination of translations, reflections, and rotations to make the magic square design.

ADDITIONAL ACTIVITIES

Begin with an nth order magic square written in an n x n array of squares (see Figure 6-9). Express each entry in the magic square in mod m, where $m \leq n$ (see Figure 6-10). Assign different colors or patterned squares to the elements in mod m. Substitute the colors or patterned squares for the entries in the magic square to create a basic design pattern (see Figure 6-11). Look for symmetries in this basic design pattern. Use combinations of reflections, translations, and rotations to create larger magic square designs.

10	3	15	6
5	16	4	9
8	13	1	12
11	2	14	7

Figure 6-9
Fourth Order
Magic Square

2	3	3	2
1	0	0	1
0	1	1	0
3	2	2	3

Figure 6-10
Entries Changed
to Mod 4

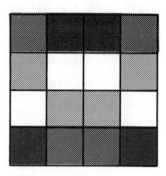

Figure 6-11
Basic
Design Pattern

Figure 6-12

116

CHAPTER 7

POLYGON DESIGNS FROM FIBONACCI NUMBERS

In previous chapters, we used many kinds of polygons in the design grids. There, we focused on creating designs by coloring the tessellating polygons according to mathematical patterns. In this chapter, we will explore some designs which can be created within single polygons, using numbers from a special sequence known as the *Fibonacci sequence*. We will make division marks on the sides of polygons, join the division marks according to certain rules, and shade in the resulting designs. As culminating activities for this chapter, we will combine these individually designed polygons and use them as tangrams, Pattern Blocks, and faces of polyhedra.

FIBONACCI SEQUENCE

The medieval mathematician Fibonacci (1180–1250), also called Leonard of Pisa, discovered this sequence of numbers. He initiated an exploration of its special properties and applications, and this exploration still continues today.

The first two numbers in the Fibonacci sequence are 1 and 1. Each successive number is the sum of the two preceding numbers in the sequence. Take the beginning of the sequence, for example:

$$1, \quad 1, \quad 2, \quad 3, \quad 5, \quad \ldots$$
$$1 + 1 = 2$$
$$1 + 2 = 3$$
$$2 + 3 = 5 \qquad \text{and so on.}$$

PALINDROMIC SEQUENCES

There are infinitely many numbers in the Fibonacci sequence, but we will use only finite sets of the numbers to create our polygon designs. We will work with a special finite sequence of numbers called a *palindromic sequence*. A palindromic sequence reads the same from left to right as from right to left. It can be thought of as being symmetric about the center of the sequence: the left half of the sequence is the mirror image of the right half (Figure 7-1). The symmetry of this number sequence will be seen in the symmetry of our designs.

1, 1, 2, 3, 5, 3, 2, 1, 1

Figure 7-1
Palindromic Sequence

DIVIDING THE SIDES OF A POLYGON

To begin a polygon design, we divide each side of the polygon into segments corresponding in length to a palindromic sequence of Fibonacci numbers. Figures 7-2 and 7-3 illustrate how we divide a side of a polygon into segments corresponding in length to this sequence: 1, 1, 2, 3, 5, 3, 2, 1, 1. First, we add all the numbers in the sequence to find the total number of units into which the side must be divided. The sum of the numbers in this sequence is 19, so we divide $\overline{AB}$ into 19 parts (Figure 7-2). Then we mark off segments corresponding in length to the numbers in the palindromic sequence by placing division points on $\overline{AB}$ (Figure 7-3).

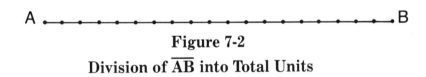

Figure 7-2

Division of $\overline{AB}$ into Total Units

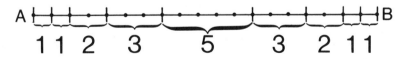

Figure 7-3

Division of $\overline{AB}$ into Segments
Corresponding in Length to
Palindromic Sequence Numbers

119

ACTIVITY: FIBONACCI NUMBERS, PALINDROMIC SEQUENCES, AND DIVISIONS OF LINE SEGMENTS

1. List the next eight terms of the Fibonacci sequence, using this rule: Every number in the Fibonacci sequence, except the first two, is the sum of the preceding two numbers in the sequence.

   1, 1, 2, 3, 5, ____ , ____ , ____ , ____ , ____ , ____ , ____ , ____

2. Complete these finite sequences so that they are palindromic; that is, so that they read the same from left to right as from right to left. (The center number of the sequence is underlined.)

   a. 1, 1, 2, 3, 5, <u>8,</u> ____ , ____ , ____ , ____ , ____ ,

   b. 3, 2, 1, <u>1,</u> ____ , ____ , ____

   c. 13, 8, 5, 3, 2, 1, <u>1,</u> ____ , ____ , ____ , ____ , ____ , ____

   d. 5, 3, 2, 1, 1, 1, 2, 3, <u>5,</u> ____ , ____ , ____ , ____ , ____ , ____ , ____ , ____

3. Divide each of the line segments below into segments with lengths corresponding to the sequence of numbers given.

   a. 1, 1, 2, 3, 2, 1, 1,

M   N

   b. 4, 5, 3, 2, 1, 1, 1, 2, 3, 5, 4

O   P

   c. 2, 1, 1, 1, 2, 3, 5, 3, 2, 1, 1, 1, 2

Q   R

   d. 5, 3, 2, 1, 1, 1, 2, 3, 5

S   T

ACTIVITY: PARALLEL DIVISIONS OF A SQUARE

In Figure 7-4, each side of the square ABCD has been divided into segments with lengths corresponding to this sequence of numbers: 1.5, 2, 1, 1, 1, 2, 1.5. (Notice that the first and last terms in the sequence are each half of the Fibonacci number 3. When you look at the complete square, you can see that the combined lengths of the two small segments at each vertex of the square is 3.) Corresponding points on $\overline{AB}$ and $\overline{DC}$ have been connected by straight line segments which are parallel to sides $\overline{AD}$ and $\overline{BC}$. Similarly, the corresponding points on $\overline{AD}$ and $\overline{BC}$ have been connected by straight line segments which are parallel to $\overline{AB}$ and $\overline{DC}$. The result is a checkerboard-like pattern consisting of square and rectangular regions.

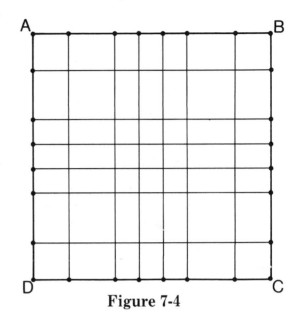

Figure 7-4

By shading in some of the regions, we can create a pleasing design in the square. The rule we will follow is that no two adjacent regions may be shaded (or that no two adjacent regions may be the same color).

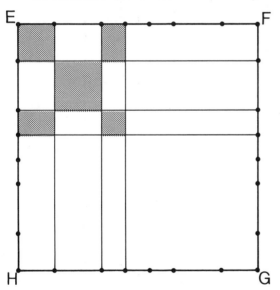

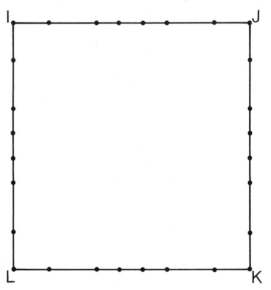

1. The sides of squares EFGH and IJKL have been divided in the same pattern as square ABCD. Finish drawing the line segments between the corresponding points on opposite sides of these squares.
2. A checkerboard-like pattern of shading has been started on square EFGH, with the square region in the corner at E shaded in. Finish shading square EFGH in this pattern.
3. Now shade square IJKL in a checkerboard-like pattern, but leave blank the square region in the corner at I. How do the two shading patterns compare?
4. How many lines of symmetry can you find in your completed design in square IJKL? _____

ACTIVITY: PARALLEL DIVISIONS OF A SQUARE

1. Sides $\overline{MN}$ and $\overline{PO}$ of square MNOP below have been divided into segments corresponding in length to this sequence of numbers: 2, 1, 1, 1, 2, 3, 5, 3, 2, 1, 1, 1, 2. Corresponding points on sides $\overline{MN}$ and $\overline{PO}$ have been connected by straight line segments.

   Divide sides $\overline{MP}$ and $\overline{NO}$ in the same way and connect corresponding points by straight line segments.

2. Color the rectangular and square regions formed by the vertical and horizontal lines. Using two colors (or blank and shaded regions), color square MNOP like a checkerboard. Remember the rule that no two adjacent regions may be the same color (or shaded).

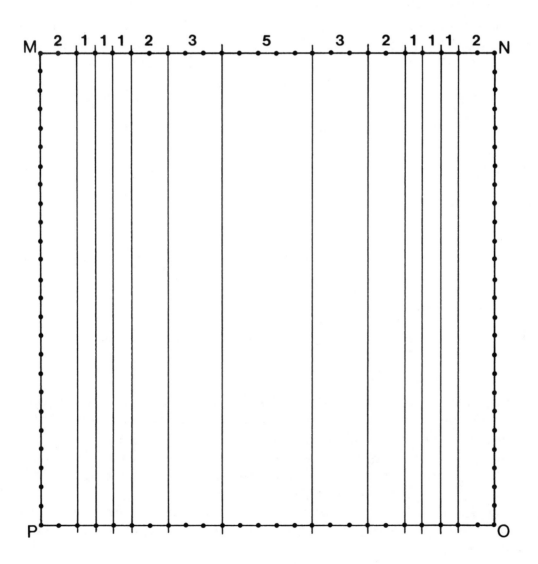

ACTIVITY: PARALLEL DIVISIONS OF A RHOMBUS

1. Sides $\overline{AB}$ and $\overline{DC}$ of rhombus ABCD have been divided into segments corresponding in length to this sequence of numbers: 4, 5, 3, 2, 1, 1, 1, 2, 3, 5, 4. (Notice that the first and last term, 4, is half of the Fibonacci number 8. When you look at the complete rhombus you can see that the combined length of the two small segments at each vertex of the rhombus is 8.) Corresponding points on $\overline{AB}$ and $\overline{DC}$ have been connected by straight line segments.

   Divide sides $\overline{AD}$ and $\overline{BC}$ in the same way and connect corresponding points by straight line segments.

2. Make a black and white checkerboard-like design by coloring the regions formed. Start with the region in the corner at A and color it black.

3. Identify the lines of symmetry in your finished design.

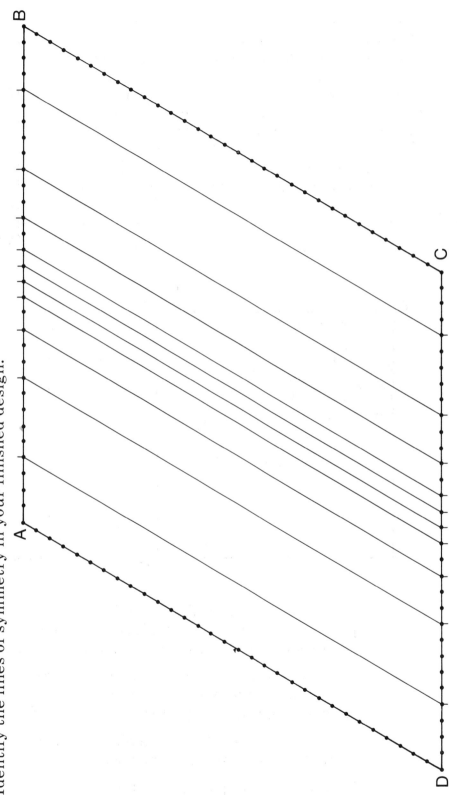

ACTIVITY: DIAGONAL DIVISIONS OF A SQUARE

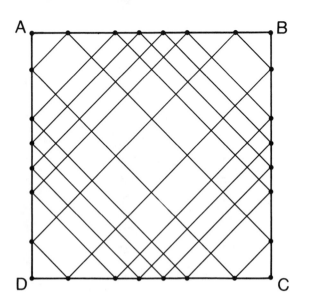

Each side of square ABCD has been divided into segments corresponding in length to this sequence of numbers: 1.5, 2, 1, 1, 1, 2, 1.5. Points of $\overline{AD}$ have been connected to corresponding points on $\overline{AB}$ by line segments which are parallel to diagonal $\overline{BD}$ of the square. Similarly, the corresponding points of $\overline{CD}$ and $\overline{CB}$, of $\overline{BA}$ and $\overline{BC}$, and of $\overline{DA}$ and $\overline{DC}$ have been connected by straight line segments. The result is a variation of the checkerboard-like pattern.

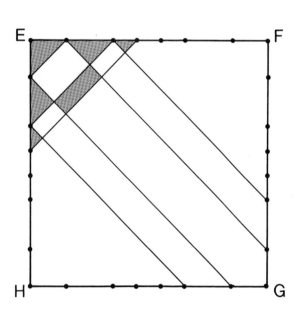

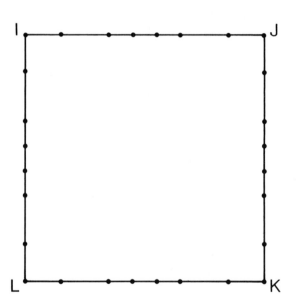

1. The sides of squares EFGH and IJKL have been divided in the same pattern as square ABCD. Finish drawing the segments between the corresponding points on adjacent sides of these squares.

2. A checkerboard-like pattern of shading has been started on square EFGH, with the region in the corner at E shaded in. Finish shading square EFGH in this pattern.

3. Now shade square IJKL in a checkerboard-like pattern, but leave blank the region in the corner at I.

4. How are the two patterns different?
   Which pattern do you prefer?
   Identify the lines of symmetry in the design in square IJKL.

ACTIVITY: DIAGONAL DIVISIONS OF A SQUARE

1. Side $\overline{AB}$ of the square ABCD has been divided into segments corresponding in length to this sequence of numbers: 4, 5, 3, 2, 1, 1, 1, 2, 3, 5, 4. Divide the other 3 sides of the square in the same pattern.

2. Connect with straight line segments the corresponding points on the adjacent sides of the square: $\overline{AB}$ and $\overline{AD}$, $\overline{BA}$ and $\overline{BC}$, $\overline{CB}$ and $\overline{CD}$, $\overline{DC}$ and $\overline{DA}$. The straight line segments that you draw will be parallel to one of the diagonals of the square. Do *not* draw diagonals $\overline{AC}$ and $\overline{BD}$.

3. Shade the regions in a checkerboard-like pattern, using one color and white. Begin by shading in the region in the corner at A.

ACTIVITY: DIAGONAL DIVISIONS OF A RHOMBUS

1. In the rhombus below, $\overline{AB}$ has been divided into segments corresponding in length to this sequence of numbers: 4, 5, 3, 2, 1, 1, 1, 2, 3, 5, 4. Divide the other three sides of the rhombus in the same pattern.

2. Connect with straight line segments the corresponding points on the adjacent sides of the rhombus: $\overline{AB}$ and $\overline{AD}$, $\overline{BA}$ and $\overline{BC}$, $\overline{CB}$ and $\overline{CD}$, $\overline{DC}$ and $\overline{DA}$. The segments that you draw will be parallel to one of the diagonals of the rhombus. Do *not* draw the diagonals $\overline{AC}$ and $\overline{BD}$.

3. Color the various regions in a checkerboard-like pattern, using two colors.

4. How many lines of symmetry does your finished design have? _____

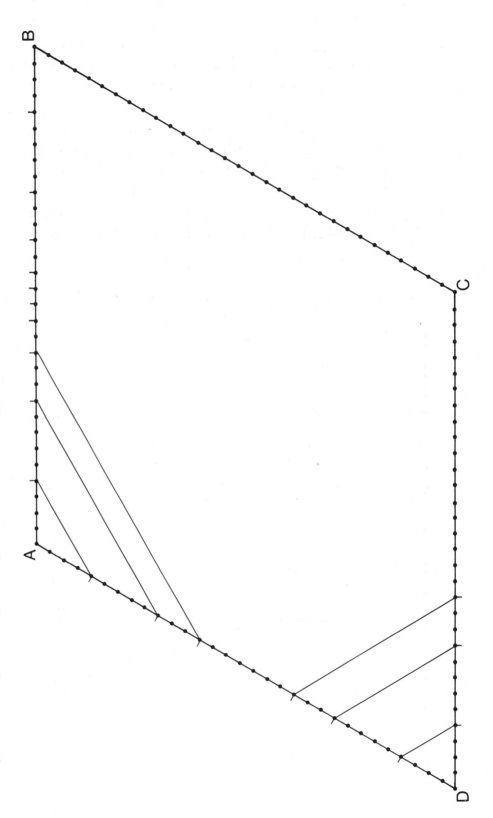

126

ACTIVITY: PARALLEL DIVISIONS OF A TRIANGLE

In Figure 7-5, each side of triangle ABC has been divided into segments corresponding in length to this sequence of numbers: 1.5, 2, 1, 1, 1, 2, 1.5. Points of $\overline{BA}$ have been connected to corresponding points on $\overline{BC}$ by straight line segments which are parallel to side $\overline{CA}$. Similarly, points of $\overline{CB}$ have been connected to corresponding points of $\overline{CA}$ by segments which are parallel to $\overline{BA}$; and points of $\overline{AC}$ have been connected to corresponding points of $\overline{AB}$ by segments which are parallel to $\overline{CB}$. The result is a variation of the checkerboard-like pattern.

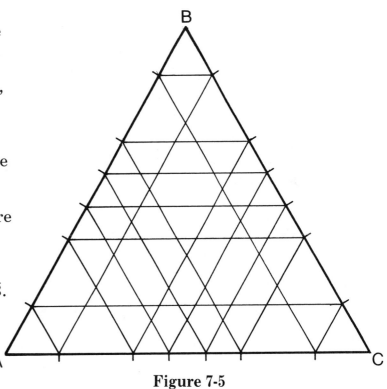

Figure 7-5

1. The sides of triangle DEF have been divided in the same pattern as triangle ABC. Finish connecting the corresponding points on the sides of the triangle to make a copy of the pattern drawn in triangle ABC.

2. Complete the checkerboard-like pattern of shading.

3. How many lines of symmetry does the finished design have?

———

127

ACTIVITY: PARALLEL DIVISIONS OF A TRIANGLE

1. In equilateral triangle ABC, the base $\overline{AC}$ has been divided into segments corresponding in length to this sequence of numbers: 4, 5, 3, 2, 1, 1, 1, 2, 3, 5, 4. Divide sides $\overline{BA}$ and $\overline{BC}$ in the same pattern as $\overline{AC}$.

2. Connect with straight line segments the corresponding points on the sides of the triangle: $\overline{AB}$ and $\overline{AC}$, $\overline{BC}$ and $\overline{BA}$, $\overline{CB}$ and $\overline{CA}$. Each of the line segments that you draw between points on two sides of the triangle will be parallel to the third side of the triangle.

3. Color the various regions of the triangle in a checkerboard-like pattern, using two colors. If you choose to use one color and white, begin by shading in a region in the corner at A, B, or C.

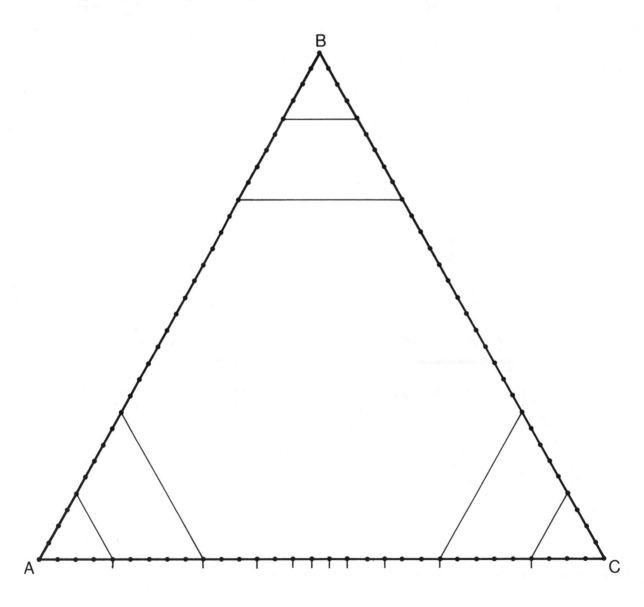

ACTIVITY: PARALLEL DIVISIONS OF A PENTAGON

1. In pentagon ABCDE, $\overline{AE}$ and $\overline{CD}$ have been divided into segments corresponding in length to this sequence of numbers: 4, 5, 3, 2, 1, 1, 1, 2, 3, 5, 4. Divide sides $\overline{AB}$, $\overline{BC}$, and $\overline{DE}$ in the same pattern.

2. Study the way in which the straight line segments have been drawn between corresponding points on $\overline{AE}$ and $\overline{CD}$. Each of these segments is parallel to $\overline{ED}$, which is the side touching both sides $\overline{AE}$ and $\overline{CD}$. Now complete the pattern of line segments, joining the corresponding points on $\overline{AE}$ and $\overline{BC}$, $\overline{AB}$ and $\overline{DC}$, $\overline{BC}$ and $\overline{ED}$, and $\overline{ED}$ and $\overline{AB}$. Notice that the segments you draw are parallel to the side of the pentagon that touches the two sides you are connecting.

3. Use black and another color to color the various regions in a checkerboard-like pattern. Start with black in the region at vertex E.

4. How many lines of symmetry does your finished design have? _____

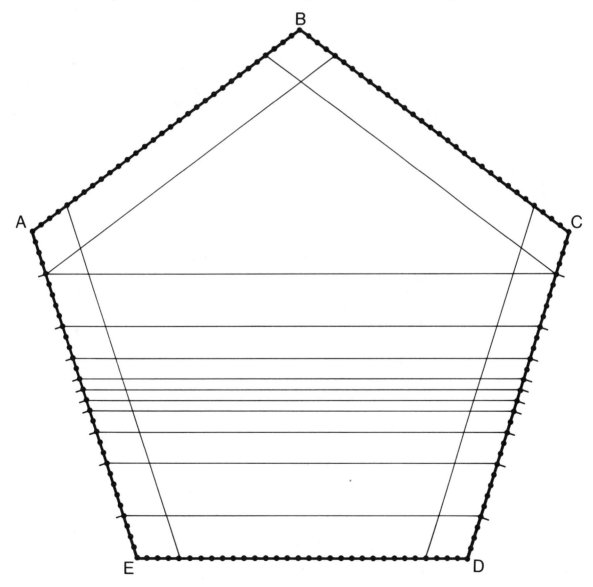

ACTIVITY: PARALLEL DIVISIONS OF A HEXAGON

1. Each side of hexagon ABCDEF has been divided into segments with lengths corresponding to this sequence of numbers: 4, 5, 3, 2, 1, 1, 1, 2, 3, 5, 4. Division points on $\overline{AB}$ have been connected by straight line segments with corresponding points on $\overline{FE}$. Each segment is parallel to $\overline{AF}$. Complete the pattern of line segments, joining the corresponding points on $\overline{AF}$ and $\overline{BC}$, $\overline{AB}$ and $\overline{DC}$, $\overline{BC}$ and $\overline{ED}$, $\overline{CD}$ and $\overline{FE}$, and $\overline{DE}$ and $\overline{AF}$. Notice that the segments you draw between any two sides of the hexagon are parallel to the side that touches the two sides you are connecting.

2. Color the various regions in a checkerboard-like pattern, using black and white. Start with black in the region at each vertex of the hexagon.

3. How many lines of symmetry does the finished design have? _____

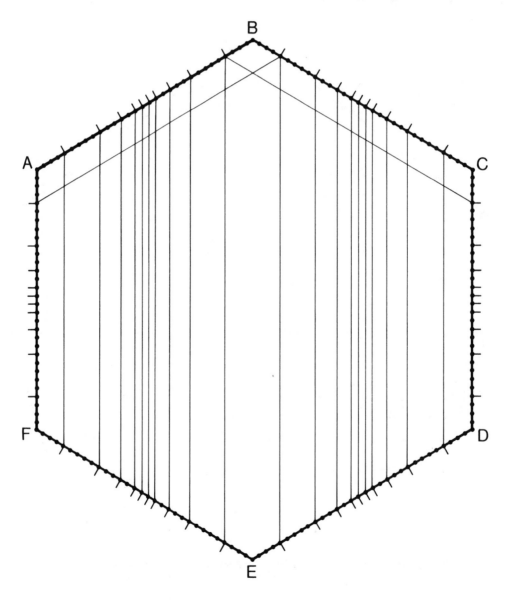

ACTIVITY: DIAGONAL DIVISIONS OF AN OCTAGON

1. Each side of octagon ABCDEFGH has been divided into segments with lengths corresponding to this sequence of numbers: 1.5, 2, 1, 1, 1, 2, 1.5. Points on $\overline{BA}$ and $\overline{BC}$ have been connected with straight line segments to corresponding points of $\overline{FG}$ and $\overline{FE}$. Complete the pattern by connecting the points on $\overline{AH}$ and $\overline{AB}$ with corresponding points on $\overline{EF}$ and $\overline{ED}$; the points on $\overline{CB}$ and $\overline{CD}$ with corresponding points on $\overline{GH}$ and $\overline{GF}$; and the points of $\overline{DC}$ and $\overline{DE}$ with corresponding points on $\overline{HA}$ and $\overline{HG}$.

2. Color the various regions in a checkerboard-like pattern, using black and white. Start with black at each vertex of the octagon.

3. How many lines of symmetry are in the finished design? _____

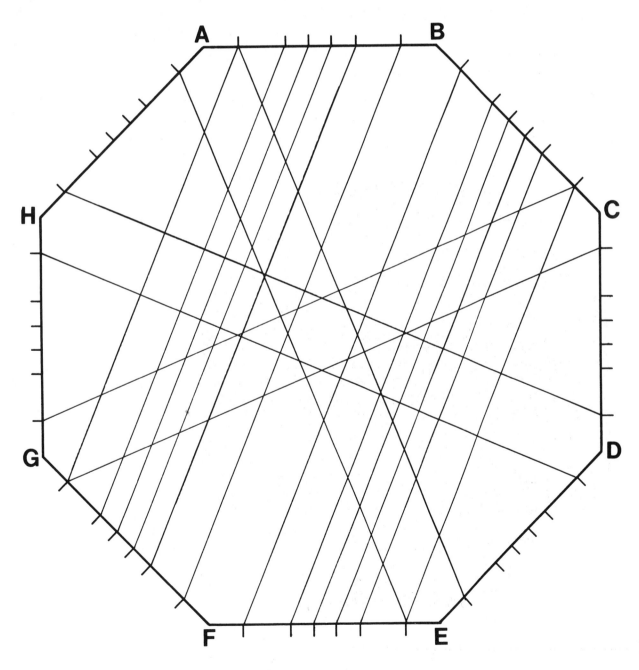

131

ACTIVITY: DIAGONAL DIVISIONS OF AN OCTAGON

1. On a large sheet of paper, trace this incomplete octagon outline ABCDEF. Rotate this pattern 180° in a clockwise direction, until $\overline{AB}$ is in the place of $\overline{EF}$. Finish tracing the octagon. Continuing the sequence of letters that mark the points, label the new vertices G and H.

2. Copy the division points from each side of the octagon pattern onto your own octagon. Each side has been divided into segments with lengths corresponding to this sequence of numbers: 4, 5, 3, 2, 1, 1, 1, 2, 3, 5, 4.

3. Draw straight line segments connecting the points on $\overline{BA}$ and $\overline{BC}$ with corresponding points on $\overline{FG}$ and $\overline{FE}$; the points on $\overline{AH}$ and $\overline{AB}$ with corresponding points of $\overline{EF}$ and $\overline{ED}$; the points on $\overline{CB}$ and $\overline{CD}$ with corresponding points on $\overline{GH}$ and $\overline{GF}$; and the points of $\overline{DC}$ and $\overline{DE}$ with corresponding points on $\overline{HA}$ and $\overline{HG}$.

4. Color the regions in a checkerboard-like pattern, using black and white. Start with black at each vertex of the octagon. The result should be a very attractive octagon similar to the one in Figure 7-6.

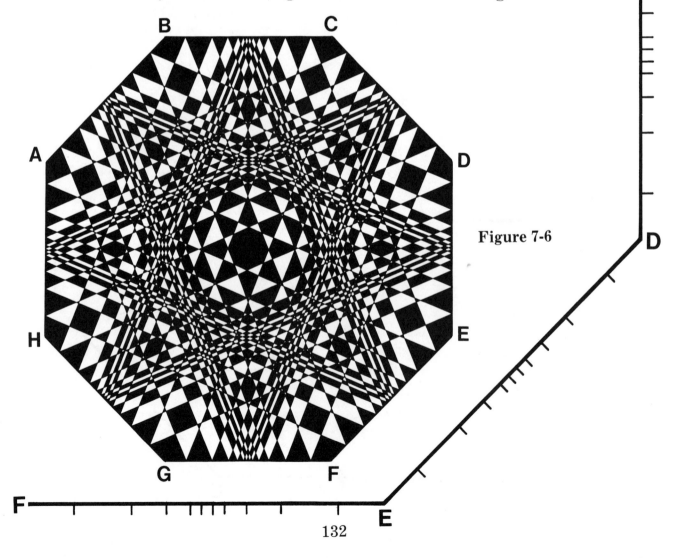

Figure 7-6

FIBONACCI-DESIGN PATTERN BLOCKS

The design on each of the six basic Pattern Block shapes (equilateral triangle, trapezoid, square, hexagon, and two distinct rhombi) shown on the next page was made by dividing the sides of the shapes in lengths corresponding to palindromic sequences of Fibonacci numbers. Because of the geometric relationships among these six Pattern Block shapes, they can be used to create tessellation designs. The use of Fibonacci designs on the basic shapes allows us to create exciting and complex designs with them very easily.

The two designs shown in Figures 7-7 and 7-8 were made from Fibonacci-design Pattern Blocks. The illustrations are from *Pattern Blocks Coloring Book*.* The diagrams below the designs show the Pattern Block shapes that were combined to create the designs.

Figure 7-7   **Figure 7-8**

*Marian Pasternack and Linda Silvey, *Pattern Blocks Coloring Book* (Palo Alto, California: Creative Publications, Inc., 1974).

ACTIVITY: FIBONACCI-DESIGN PATTERN BLOCKS

Make six or more copies of this page and paste them on cardboard, or duplicate the page on stiff paper. Cut out the Pattern Blocks and fit them together into tessellation designs.

Triangle

Trapezoid

Rhombus

Square

Hexagon

Rhombus

FIBONACCI-DESIGN TANGRAMS

The tangram is a seven-piece puzzle cut from a square. The pieces (as shown in Figure 7-9) are the following polygons: 1 and 2 are large isosceles right triangles; 3 and 5 are small isosceles right triangles; 7 is a medium isosceles right triangle; 4 is a square; and 6 is a parallelogram.

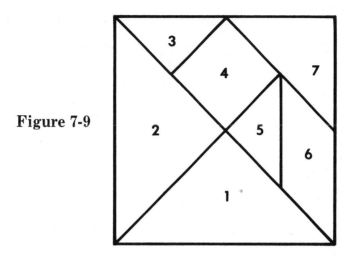

Figure 7-9

Although there are seven different pieces in the tangram, pieces 1, 2, 4, 6, and 7 could be constructed from basic triangles, if triangle 3 or 5 were used as the basic unit triangle. This can be seen in Figure 7-10.

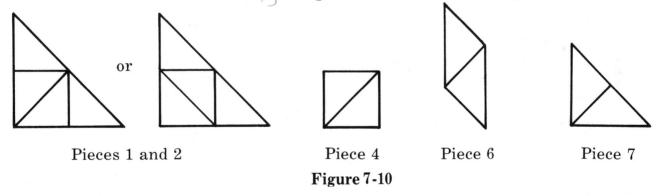

Pieces 1 and 2   Piece 4   Piece 6   Piece 7

Figure 7-10

The tangram pieces shown on **pages 137 and 138** have been made from a combination of small isosceles triangles which have a Fibonacci-design pattern on them. The tangram square has two different designs, one made by a combination of the two small triangles, and the other made by diagonal divisions of the square.

Challenge!

Analyze the Fibonacci-design patterns on the small triangle and the square. Show how the other shapes were formed from combinations of the small triangles.

ACTIVITY: FIBONACCI-DESIGN TANGRAMS

1. Make a copy of pages 137 and 138. Cut out the two shapes in each outlined section and glue the two shapes together back-to-back. This will give you the seven tangram puzzle pieces with a Fibonacci-design pattern on each side.

   Which pieces have a different design on front and back?

2. Use the seven pieces of the tangram to form each of the 13 convex polygons shown below.

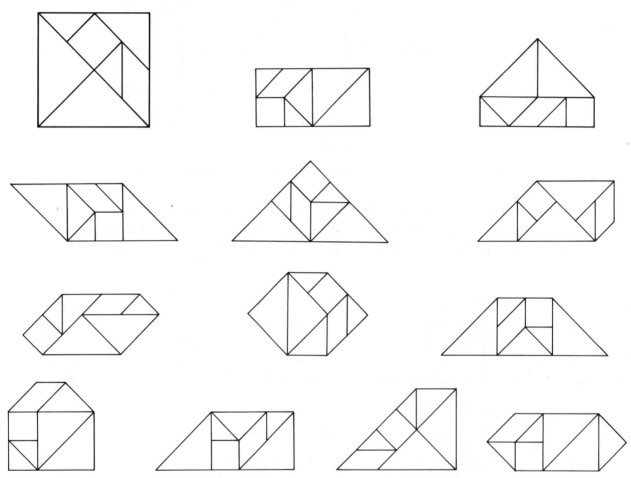

3. After forming each of the polygons, rotate or flip over the square piece and /or flip over the large triangular pieces to change the design.

4. How many different designs can you find for each polygon?
   How many lines of symmetry does each design have?
   Which designs have rotational symmetry?

ACTIVITY: FIBONACCI-DESIGN POLYHEDRA

Interesting polyhedra models can be constructed of polygons which have Fibonacci-design patterns on them. The networks for three of the regular polyhedra are given on pages 140-142.

1. Construct the polyhedra from the networks given. Follow these general instructions:

   a. Duplicate or paste a copy of the polyhedron design network on lightweight tagboard or a file folder.
   b. Cut out the network along the outside line.
   c. Score the edges (using a compass point or a craft knife) between faces and between a face and a flap.
   d. Fold (mountain folds) on the scored edges so that the design is on the outside.
   e. Glue the flaps under adjoining edges to form the polyhedron.

2. After you have constructed the polyhedra from the networks given, to make your own networks for other regular and semiregular polyhedra, using the polygon patterns on page A-22.

Fibonacci-Design Hexahedron or Cube

Fibonacci-Design Dodecahedron

Fibonacci-Design Icosahedron

CHAPTER 8

SPIROGRAM DESIGNS FROM NUMBER SEQUENCES

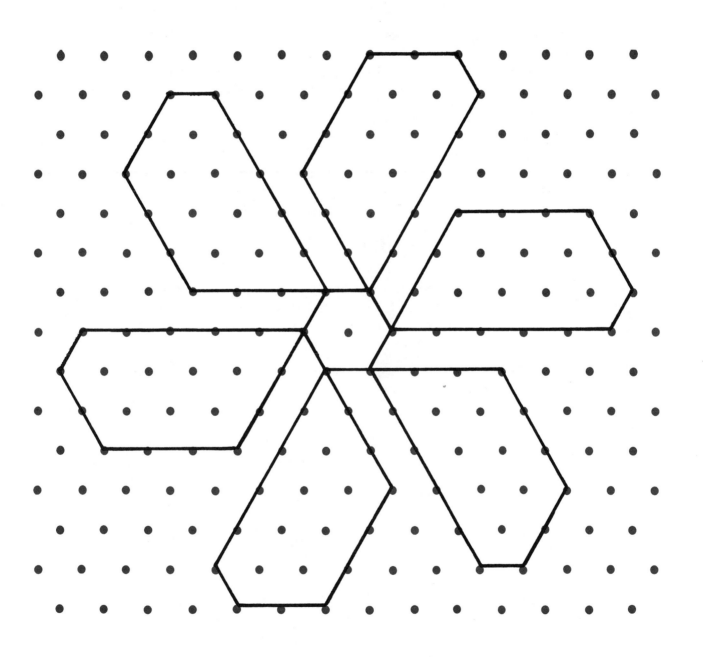

SPIROGRAMS

Spirals are one of the most beautiful of all forms that we see in nature and art. They can be created in a variety of ways—from continuously curved lines or from a series of straight line segments.

Spirograms, as the name suggests, are spirals formed by a sequence of straight line segments corresponding in length to a sequence of natural numbers. The line segments are turned successively according to a given angle measure.

Spirograms are drawn using infinite sequences of counting numbers, even numbers, odd numbers, Fibonacci numbers, and many others.

To create a spirogram design, we choose a sequence of numbers that determines the lengths of the segments comprising the spirogram, and an angle measure that specifies how much successive segments are to be turned. We will use dot paper for drawing the spirograms because it provides handy units of length and facilitates drawing angles.

As we draw the spirograms in the following activities, we will concentrate on angle measures of 90°, 60°, and 120°. We will use square and isometric dot paper for drawing the designs. In all activities, we will make the turns in a counterclockwise direction.

NINETY DEGREE SPIROGRAMS

First, we will explore spirograms made by turning successive segments 90° counterclockwise, with the lengths of the successive segments corresponding to an infinite sequence of counting numbers. The four examples below illustrate the technique of drawing spirograms.

Example 1: Draw a spirogram for the sequence 1, 1, 1, 1, . . . , using 90° counterclockwise turns.

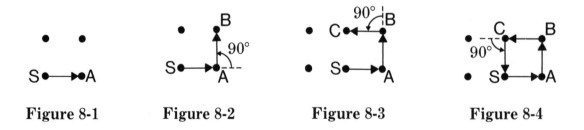

Figure 8-1   Figure 8-2   Figure 8-3   Figure 8-4

Square dot paper allows us to make 90° turns and to draw segments one unit long very easily. The distance between any two vertical or horizontal dots represents one unit. The sequence indicates that each of the segments drawn will be one unit long.

144

First, we choose a starting point S (Figure 8-1). We draw $\overline{SA}$ one unit long, horizontally to the right. At A, we turn 90° counterclockwise and draw a segment one unit long, ending at point B (Figure 8-2). At B, we turn 90° counterclockwise and draw a segment one unit long, ending at point C (Figure 8-3). At C, we turn 90° counterclockwise and draw a segment one unit long, ending at the starting point S (Figure 8-4).

If we were to continue turning and drawing segments one unit long, we would merely retrace the path already drawn. Hence Figure 8-4 is the spirogram for the infinite sequence 1, 1, 1, 1, . . . , using 90° turns. Notice that all the numbers in the infinite sequence are the same, and that we drew four segments before returning to the starting point.

Example 2: Draw a spirogram for the sequence 1, 2, 1, 2, 1, 2, . . . , using 90° counterclockwise turns.

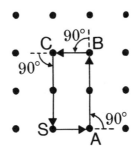

Figure 8-5

The sequence indicates that we will draw a segment one unit long, followed by a segment two units long, followed by a segment one unit long, followed by a segment two units long, and so on.

We choose a starting point S. We draw $\overline{SA}$ one unit long, horizontally to the right. At A, we turn 90° counterclockwise and draw a segment two units long ($\overline{AB}$). At B, we turn 90° counterclockwise and draw a segment one unit long ($\overline{BC}$). At C, we turn 90° counterclockwise and draw a segment two units long ($\overline{CS}$).

If we were to continue drawing segments according to the pattern given for this spirogram, we would merely retrace the quadrilateral shown in Figure 8-5. Notice that the infinite sequence consists of repetitions of the number pattern 1-2, and also that we used this number pattern twice before we returned to the starting point.

145

Example 3: Draw a spirogram for the sequence 1, 2, 3, 1, 2, 3, ..., using 90° counterclockwise turns.

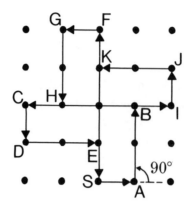

Figure 8-6

The sequence indicates that we will draw segments one unit, two units, and three units long, in that order, over and over again. Figure 8-6 shows the completed spirogram. The starting point is S and the arrows indicate the direction in which the segments are drawn. Trace the outline with your finger to verify the pattern.

Notice that the infinite sequence consists of the pattern 1-2-3 repeated again and again, and also that the sequence of three segments is drawn four times before we return to the starting point.

Example 4: Draw a spirogram for the sequence 1, 2, 3, 4, 1, 2, 3, 4, ..., using 90° counterclockwise turns.

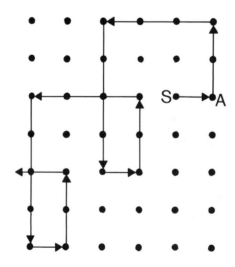

Figure 8-7

146

The sequence indicates that we will draw segments one, two, three, and four units long, in that order, over and over again. Figure 8-7 shows a part of the spirogram.

Notice that the infinite sequence consists of the number pattern 1-2-3-4 repeated again and again, and that the sequence of segments will never return to the starting point. This type of spirogram is called an *open* spirogram.

TERMINOLOGY AND NOTATION

A spirogram is determined by the turn angle measure and the number sequence given. It will be understood that turns are counterclockwise. The infinite number sequences are made of repetitions of a finite sequence of numbers which we will call the *basic pattern* for the spirogram. The number of distinct numbers in the basic pattern is termed the *order* of the spirogram.

The notation given below is a compact way of describing spirograms.

$90°S_{1,2}$ indicates a spirogram of order 2 with basic pattern 1-2. The infinite sequence is 1, 2, 1, 2, 1, 2, . . . , and the turns are each 90° counterclockwise.

$60°S_{1,3,5,7}$ indicates a spirogram of order 4 with basic pattern 1-3-5-7. The infinite sequence is 1, 3, 5, 7, 1, 3, 5, 7, . . . , and the turns are each 60° counterclockwise.

When drawing spirograms $90°S_1$, $90°S_{1,2}$, and $90°S_{1,2,3}$ (see examples 1, 2, and 3), we returned to the starting point S. The number of times the basic pattern is used to return to the starting point S is called the *repetition factor*. The repetition factor for $90°S_1$ is four; for $90°S_{1,2}$ it is two, and for $90°S_{1,2,3}$ it is four. The spirogram $90°S_{1,2,3,4}$ never returns to the starting point S.

ACTIVITY: 90° SPIROGRAMS, NATURAL NUMBERS

1. Draw the spirograms for the sequences of natural numbers given below. The starting point S and the unit length are given in each case. Use 90° counterclockwise turns.

$90°S_1$ $90°S_{1,2}$ $90°S_{1,2,3}$ $90°S_{1,2,3,4}$

$90°S_{1,2,...,5}$ $90°S_{1,2,...,6}$

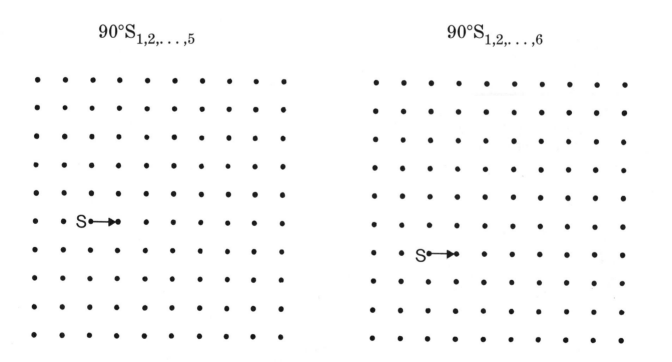

ACTIVITY: 90° SPIROGRAMS, NATURAL NUMBERS (continued)

$90°S_{1,2,\ldots,7}$ $\qquad\qquad\qquad$ $90°S_{1,2,\ldots,8}$

2. Study the spirograms in the activity above and complete Table 1.

Table 1
90° Spirograms, Natural Numbers

Spirogram	Order	Basic Pattern	Return to S? Yes	No	Number of Repetitions of Basic Pattern
$90°S_1$	1	1	X		4
$90°S_{1,2}$	2	1-2	X		2
$90°S_{1,2,3}$					
$90°S_{1,2,3,4}$	4	1-2-3-4		X	does not return
$90°S_{1,2,\ldots,5}$					
$90°S_{1,2,\ldots,6}$					
$90°S_{1,2,\ldots,7}$					
$90°S_{1,2,\ldots,8}$					

3. Give the order of those spirograms which do not return to the starting point. _____

149

ACTIVITY: 90° SPIROGRAMS, ODD NUMBERS

1. Draw the spirograms for the sequences of odd natural numbers given below. The starting point S and the unit length are given in each case. Use 90° counterclockwise turns.

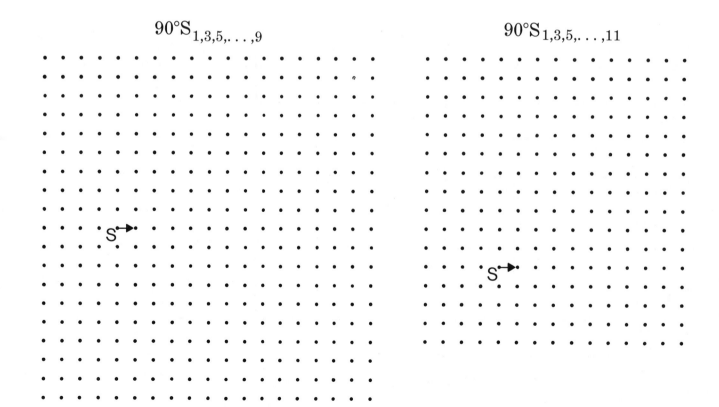

$90°S_1$ $90°S_{1,3}$ $90°S_{1,3,5}$ $90°S_{1,3,5,7}$

$90°S_{1,3,5,\ldots,9}$ $90°S_{1,3,5,\ldots,11}$

$90°S_{1,3,5,\ldots,13}$

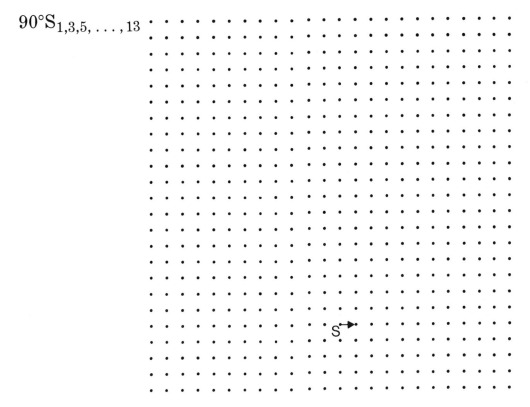

2. Study the spirograms in the activity above and complete Table 2.

Table 2
90° Spirograms, Odd Numbers

Spirogram	Order	Basic Pattern	Return to S?		Number of Repetitions of Basic Pattern
			Yes	No	
$90°S_1$	1	1	✖		4
$90°S_{1,3}$	2	1-3	✖		2
$90°S_{1,3,5}$					
$90°S_{1,3,5,7}$	4	1-3-5-7		✖	does not return
$90°S_{1,3,5,\ldots,9}$					
$90°S_{1,3,5,\ldots,11}$					
$90°S_{1,3,5,\ldots,13}$					

3. Give the order of those spirograms which do not return to the starting point S. _____

151

ACTIVITY: 90° SPIROGRAMS, EVEN NUMBERS

1. Draw the spirograms for the sequences of even natural numbers given below. The starting point S is given. The distance between two adjacent dots is the unit length. The first element of the sequence is given for each spirogram. Use 90° counterclockwise turns.

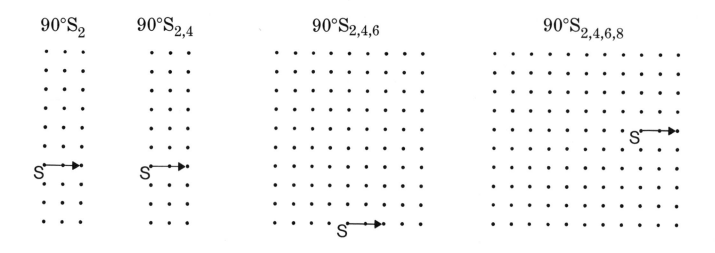

$90°S_2$ $90°S_{2,4}$ $90°S_{2,4,6}$ $90°S_{2,4,6,8}$

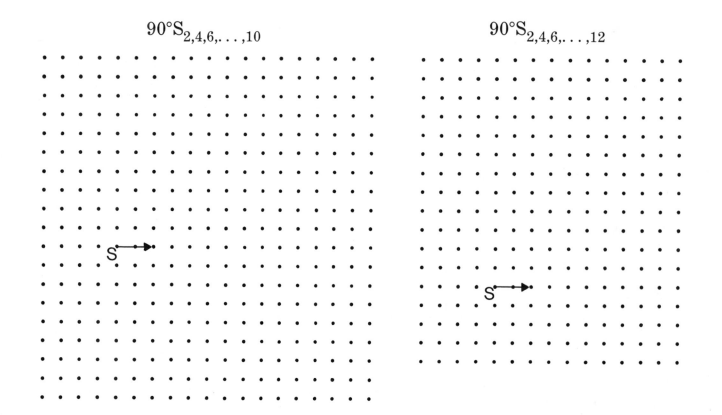

$90°S_{2,4,6,\ldots,10}$ $90°S_{2,4,6,\ldots,12}$

$$90°S_{2,4,6,\ldots,14}$$

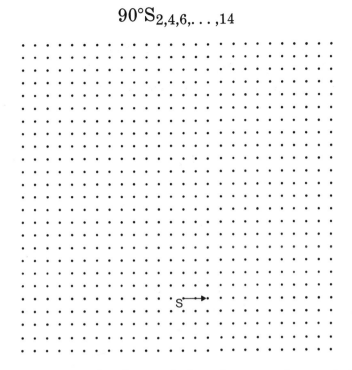

2. Study the spirograms in the activity above and complete Table 3.

Table 3
90° Spirograms, Even Numbers

Spirogram	Order	Basic Pattern	Return to S?		Number of Repetitions of Basic Pattern
			Yes	No	
$90°S_2$	1	2	X		4
$90°S_{2,4}$	2	2-4	X		2
$90°S_{2,4,6}$					
$90°S_{2,4,6,8}$					
$90°S_{2,4,6,\ldots,10}$					
$90°S_{2,4,6,\ldots,12}$					
$90°S_{2,4,6,\ldots,14}$					

3. Give the order of those spirograms which do not return to the starting point S. _____
   How do these spirograms compare with the ones in Table 1 which used the natural number sequences? _____

ACTIVITY: 90° SPIROGRAMS, FIBONACCI NUMBERS

1. Draw the spirograms for the sequences taken from the Fibonacci numbers 1, 1, 2, 3, 5, 8, 13, 21, 34, 55, ... The starting point S and the unit length are given in each case. Use 90° counterclockwise turns.

$90°S_1$

$90°S_{1,1,2}$

$90°S_{1,1,2,3}$

$90°S_{1,1,2,3,5}$

$90°S_{1,1,2,3,5,8}$

ACTIVITY: 90° SPIROGRAMS, FIBONACCI NUMBERS (continued)

$$90°S_{1,1,2,3,5,8,13}$$

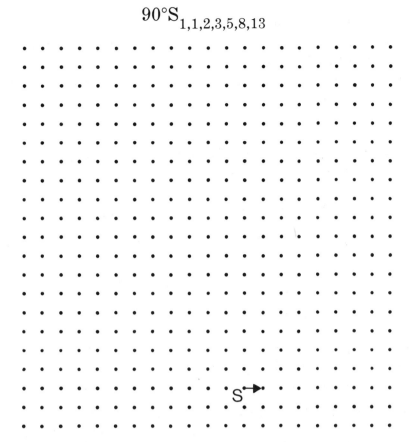

2. Study the spirograms in the activity above and complete Table 4.

Table 4
90° Spirograms, Fibonacci Numbers

Spirogram	Order	Basic Pattern	Return to S?		Number of Repetitions of Basic Pattern
			Yes	No	
$90°S_1$	1	1	X		2
$90°S_{1,1,2}$					
$90°S_{1,1,2,3}$					
$90°S_{1,1,2,3,5}$					
$90°S_{1,1,2,3,5,8}$					
$90°S_{1,1,2,3,5,8,13}$					

3. Give the order of those spirograms which do not return to the
starting point S. _____
What pattern do you see for the order of the 90° spirograms which do
not return to the starting point? _____

155

SIXTY DEGREE SPIROGRAMS

Spirograms with turns of 60° can be drawn easily and quickly on triangular or isometric dot paper. The technique is the same as that used for drawing the 90° spirograms, except that the successive segments are turned 60° counterclockwise. The following examples illustrate the procedure.

Example 1: Draw the spirogram $60°S_1$.

(Recall that this is the spirogram for the sequence 1, 1, 1, 1, . . . , using 60° counterclockwise turns.)

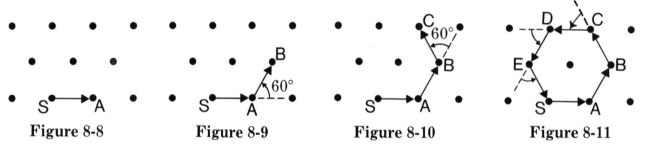

Figure 8-8   **Figure 8-9**   **Figure 8-10**   **Figure 8-11**

Triangular dot paper allows us to make 60° turns and to draw segments one unit long very easily. The sequence indicates that all the segments are to be drawn one unit long.

We choose a starting point S and draw $\overline{SA}$ one unit long, horizontally to the right (Figure 8-8). At A, we turn 60° counterclockwise and draw a segment one unit long, ending at B (Figure 8-9). At B, we turn 60° counterclockwise and draw a segment one unit long, ending at C (Figure 8-10). We continue this procedure until we return to the starting point S (Figure 8-11).

If we were to continue drawing the other elements of the sequence 1, 1, 1, 1, . . . , we would merely retrace the path already drawn. Thus, Figure 8-11 is the spirogram for the infinite sequence 1, 1, 1, 1, . . . , using 60° turns. Notice that this is an order 1 spirogram with a repetition factor of six.

Example 2: Draw the spirogram $60°S_{1,2}$.

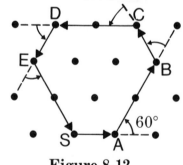

Figure 8-12

The sequence indicates that we will draw segments one unit and two units long, in that order, over and over again.

Figure 8-12 shows the completed spirogram. Notice that this is an order 2 spirogram with a repetition factor of three.

ACTIVITY: 60° SPIROGRAMS, NATURAL NUMBERS

Draw the spirograms for the sequences of natural numbers given below. The starting point S and the unit length are given in each case. Use 60° counterclockwise turns.

$60°S_1$

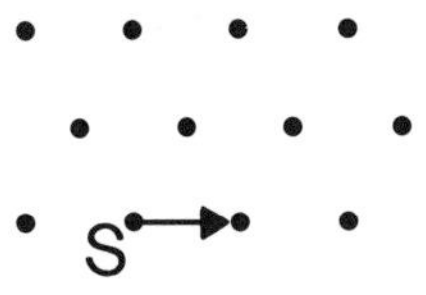

$60°S_{1,2}$

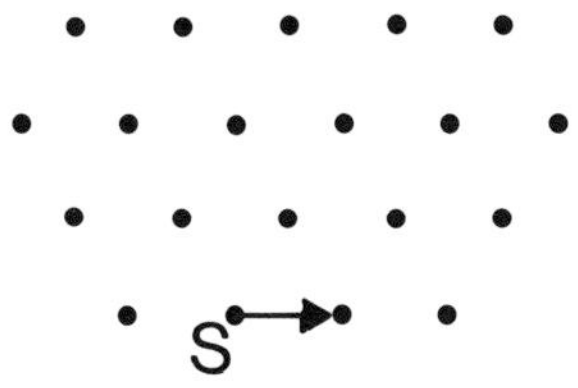

$60°S_{1,2,3,4}$

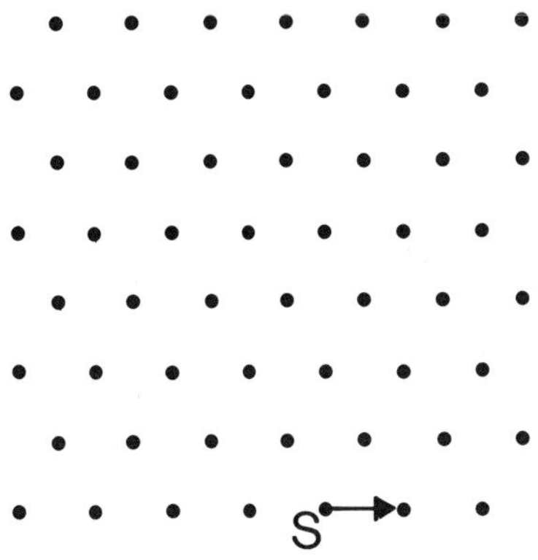

$60°S_{1,2,3}$

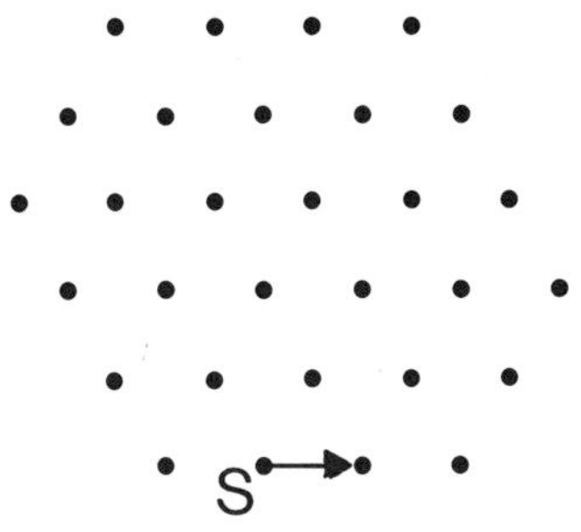

$60°S_{1,2,3,\ldots,6}$

$60°S_{1,2,3,\ldots,5}$

157

$60°S_{1,2,3\ldots,7}$

$60°S_{1,2,3,\ldots,8}$

ACTIVITY: 60° SPIROGRAMS, NATURAL NUMBERS AND ODD NUMBERS

1. Study the spirograms in the previous activity and complete the information in Table 5.

Table 5
60° Spirograms, Natural Numbers

Spirogram	Order	Basic Pattern	Return to S?		Number of Repetitions of Basic Pattern
			Yes	No	
$60°S_1$	1	1	✘		6
$60°S_{1,2}$	2	1-2	✘		3
$60°S_{1,2,3}$					
$60°S_{1,2,3,4}$					
$60°S_{1,2,\ldots,5}$					
$60°S_{1,2,\ldots,6}$	6	1-2-3-4-5-6		✘	does not return
$60°S_{1,2,\ldots,7}$					
$60°S_{1,2,\ldots,8}$					

2. Give the order of those spirograms which do not return to the starting point S. _____

3. On copies of page A-23, construct the 60° spirograms listed in Table 6. Complete the information in the table.

Table 6
60° Spirograms, Odd Numbers

Spirogram	Order	Basic Pattern	Return to S?		Number of Repetitions of Basic Pattern
			Yes	No	
$60°S_1$	1	1	✘		6
$60°S_{1,3}$					
$60°S_{1,3,5}$					
$60°S_{1,3,5,7}$					
$60°S_{1,3,5,\ldots,9}$					
$60°S_{1,3,5,\ldots,11}$	6	1-3-5-7-9-11		✘	does not return

4. Give the order of those spirograms which do not return to the starting point S. _____

159

ACTIVITY: 60° SPIROGRAMS, EVEN NUMBERS AND FIBONACCI NUMBERS

1. On copies of page A-23, construct the spirograms listed in Table 7. Complete the information in the table. (Can you predict the results before drawing the spirograms?)

Table 7
60° Spirograms, Even Numbers

Spirogram	Order	Basic Pattern	Return to S?		Number of Repetitions of Basic Pattern
			Yes	No	
$60°S_2$	1	2	X		6
$60°S_{2,4}$					
$60°S_{2,4,6}$					
$60°S_{2,4,6,8}$					
$60°S_{2,4,6,\ldots,10}$					
$60°S_{2,4,6,\ldots,12}$					

2. Give the order of those spirograms which do not return to the starting point S. _____

3. On copies of page A-23, construct the spirograms listed in Table 8. Complete the information in the table.

Table 8
60° Spirograms, Fibonacci Numbers

Spirogram	Order	Basic Pattern	Return to S?		Number of Repetitions of Basic Pattern
			Yes	No	
$60°S_1$	1	1	X		6
$60°S_{1,1,2}$					
$60°S_{1,1,2,3}$					
$60°S_{1,1,2,3,5}$					
$60°S_{1,1,2,3,5,8}$					
$60°S_{1,1,2,3,5,8,13}$	7	1-1-2-3-5-8-13	X		6

4. Give the order of those spirograms which do not return to the starting point S. _____

160

ONE HUNDRED TWENTY DEGREE SPIROGRAMS

Spirograms with turns of 120° can be drawn easily and quickly on triangular or isometric dot paper. The technique is the same as that used for drawing 90° or 60° spirograms, except that the successive segments are turned 120° counterclockwise. The following examples illustrate the procedure.

Example 1: Draw the spirogram $120°S_1$.

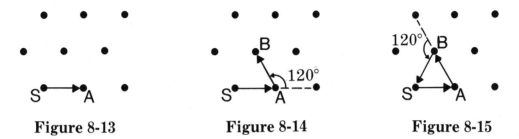

| Figure 8-13 | Figure 8-14 | Figure 8-15 |

(Recall that this is the spirogram for the sequence 1, 1, 1, 1, . . . , using 120° counterclockwise turns.)

The sequence indicates that each segment drawn will be one unit long.

We choose a starting point S and draw $\overline{SA}$ one unit long, horizontally to the right (Figure 8-13). At A, we turn 120° counterclockwise and draw a segment one unit long, ending at B (Figure 8-14). At B, we turn 120° counterclockwise and draw a segment one unit long, ending at the starting point S (Figure 8-15).

If we were to continue to draw other elements of the sequence 1, 1, 1, 1, . . . , we would merely retrace the path already drawn. Thus, Figure 8-15 is the spirogram for the infinite sequence 1, 1, 1, 1, . . . , using 120° counterclockwise turns. Notice that this is an order 1 spirogram with a repetition factor of three.

Example 2: Draw the spirogram $120°S_{1,2}$.

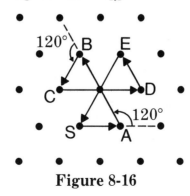

Figure 8-16

The sequence indicates that we will draw segments one unit and two units long, in that order, over and over again.

Figure 8-16 shows the completed spirogram. Notice that this is an order 2 spirogram with a repetition factor of three.

161

ACTIVITY: 120° SPIROGRAMS, NATURAL NUMBERS AND ODD NUMBERS

1. On copies of page A-23, construct the spirograms listed in Table 9. Complete the information in the table.

Table 9
120° Spirograms, Natural Numbers

Spirogram	Order	Basic Pattern	Return to S?		Number of Repetitions of Basic Pattern
			Yes	No	
$120°S_1$	1	1	X		3
$120°S_{1,2}$	2	1-2	X		3
$120°S_{1,2,3}$					
$120°S_{1,2,3,4}$					
$120°S_{1,2,\ldots,5}$					
$120°S_{1,2,\ldots,6}$					
$120°S_{1,2,\ldots,7}$					
$120°S_{1,2,\ldots,8}$					

2. Give the order of those spirograms which do not return to the starting point S. _____

3. On copies of page A-23, construct the spirograms listed in Table 10. Complete the information in the table.

Table 10
120° Spirograms, Odd Numbers

Spirogram	Order	Basic Pattern	Return to S?		Number of Repetitions of Basic Pattern
			Yes	No	
$120°S_1$	1	1	X		3
$120°S_{1,3}$					
$120°S_{1,3,5}$					
$120°S_{1,3,5,7}$					
$120°S_{1,3,5,\ldots,9}$					
$120°S_{1,3,5,\ldots,11}$					

4. Give the order of those spirograms which do not return to the starting point S. _____

ACTIVITY: 120° SPIROGRAMS, EVEN NUMBERS AND FIBONACCI NUMBERS

1. On copies of page A-23, construct the spirograms listed in Table 11. Complete the information in the table. Can you predict the results before drawing the spirograms?

Table 11
120° Spirograms, Even Numbers

Spirogram	Order	Basic Pattern	Return to S?		Number of Repetitions of Basic Pattern
			Yes	No	
$120°S_2$	1	2	✖		3
$120°S_{2,4}$					
$120°S_{2,4,6}$					
$120°S_{2,4,6,8}$					
$120°S_{2,4,6,\ldots,10}$					
$120°S_{2,4,6,\ldots,12}$					

2. Give the order of those spirograms which do not return to the starting point S. ____

3. On copies of page A-23, construct the spirograms listed in Table 12. Complete information in the table.

Table 12
120° Spirograms, Fibonacci Numbers

Spirogram	Order	Basic Pattern	Return to S?		Number of Repetitions of Basic Pattern
			Yes	No	
$120°S_1$	1	1	✖		3
$120°S_{1,1,2}$	3	1-1-2		✖	does not return
$120°S_{1,1,2,3}$					
$120°S_{1,1,2,3,5}$					
$120°S_{1,1,2,3,5,8}$					
$120°S_{1,1,2,3,5,8,13}$					

4. Give the order of those spirograms which do not return to the starting point S. ____

SUMMARY ACTIVITY: SPIROGRAMS

1. As you completed the 90°, 60°, and 120° spirograms in the previous activities, you may have noticed that there were two kinds of designs in each of the three groups: (1) closed designs in which the segments returned to the starting point, and (2) open designs in which the segments did not return to the starting point. Within each of the three groups, you may have seen a pattern that would help you predict which spirograms would be closed and which would be open. As you complete Table 13, you will see these patterns more clearly. Using information from Tables 1 through 12, fill in enough numbers for each group to help you clearly understand the patterns. You may want to draw the following spirograms to help you complete Table 13:

$$60°S_{1,2,3,...,9}, \ 60°S_{1,2,3,...,10}, \ 60°S_{1,2,3,...,11}, \ 60°S_{1,2,3,...,12},$$
$$\text{and } 120°S_{1,2,3,...,9}.$$

Table 13
Orders of Open Spirograms

For the turns listed below, no closed figure is obtained if the order number is in the sequence listed below.	
Turns	Order Number Sequence
90°	4, 8,
60°	6,
120°	3,

2. You may also have noticed, as you drew the spirograms and completed information in Tables 1 through 12, that there were certain patterns involving the repetition factor (i.e., the number of repetitions of the basic pattern necessary to return to the starting point) and the order of the spirograms within each of the three groups. Again using the information from Tables 1 through 12, complete Table 14 to clearly identify those patterns.

Table 14
Repetition Factors and Orders of Closed Spirograms

90° Spirograms:

Repetition factor is *two* if the order is in the sequence **2,** _____

Repetition factor is *four* if the order is in the sequence **1,** _____

60° Spirograms:

Repetition factor is *two* if the order is in the sequence **3,** _____

Repetition factor is *three* if the order is in the sequence **2,** _____

Repetition factor is *four* if the order is in the sequence **1,** _____

120° Spirograms:

Repetition factor is *three* if the order is in the sequence **1,** _____

ADDITIONAL ACTIVITIES

We have not exhausted the possible activities for spirograms. Below are listed a few other topics for possible investigation. Pages A-23 through A-26 of the Appendix are square and isometric dot paper of two sizes which may be used for drawing the spirograms.

1. Try drawing spirograms using clockwise turns. Begin by drawing the first segment horizontally to the *left* of your starting point. Then explore the various spirograms for combinations of clockwise and counterclockwise turns.

2. Investigate patterns such as those shown below, in which the sequence does not begin with the smallest number of the sequence. Use different angle measures.

   a. $S_{3,4,5}$ b. $S_{5,6,7}$

   c. $S_{3,1,5}$ d. $S_{2,7,5}$

3. Explore spirograms with cyclic permutations for a given order. Thus, for order 3, you can draw and study the spirograms:

   a. $S_{1,2,3}$ b. $S_{3,1,2}$

   c. $S_{2,3,1}$ d. $S_{1,3,2}$

   e. $S_{2,1,3}$ f. $S_{3,2,1}$

4. Which of the spirograms in this chapter can be used to tessellate a plane? This is an interesting topic for exploration.

5. Use your imagination and insight to create spirograms that are different from the designs in this chapter.

SOLUTIONS TO SELECTED PROBLEMS

Chapter 1

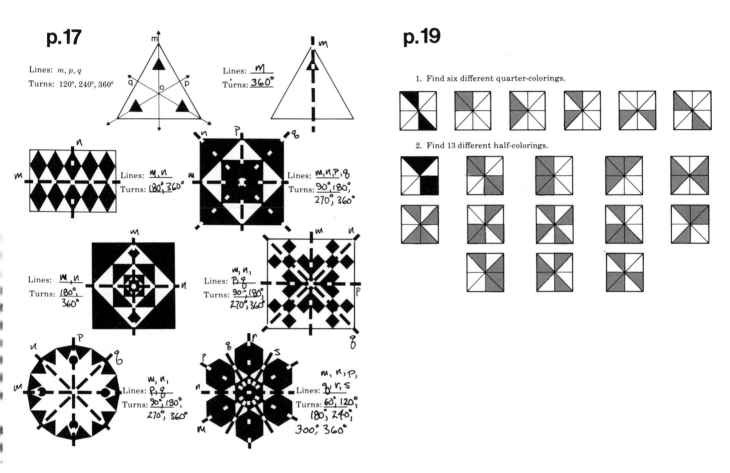

p.17

Lines: m, p, q
Turns: 120°, 240°, 360°

Lines: <u>M</u>
Turns: <u>360°</u>

Lines: <u>M, N</u>
Turns: <u>180°, 360°</u>

Lines: <u>M, N, P, Q</u>
Turns: <u>90°, 180°, 270°, 360°</u>

Lines: <u>M, N</u>
Turns: <u>180°, 360°</u>

Lines: <u>M, N, P, Q</u>
Turns: <u>90°, 180°, 270°, 360°</u>

Lines: <u>M, N, P, Q</u>
Turns: <u>90°, 180°, 270°, 360°</u>

Lines: <u>M, N, P, Q, R, S</u>
Turns: <u>60°, 120°, 180°, 240°, 300°, 360°</u>

p.19

1. Find six different quarter-colorings.

2. Find 13 different half-colorings.

Chapter 4

p.69

1. 6, 10, 15, 21, 28, 36, 45, 55

2.
Triangular Numbers	Number of Triangles
1	27
6	9
28	3
120	1

Description of pattern: 3^n, $n = 0, 1, 2, 3$

3.
Row Number	0	1	3	7	15	31	63	127	255	511	1023	2047
Number of Shaded Hexagons in Row	1	2	4	8	16	32	64	128	256	512	1024	2048

Row number pattern: $2^n - 1$
Shaded hexagon pattern: 2^n

167

p. 73

1. 1, 3, 6, 10, 15, 21, 28, 36, 45, 55

2. Triangular number: 6; number of triangles: 36

3. Triangular Numbers   Number of Triangles

        3   18

     36   3

Challenge: The next triangular number would be $\dfrac{26 \times 27}{2} = 351$.

4.

Row Number	0	1	2	5	8	17	26
Number of Shaded Hexagons in Row	1	2	3	6	9	18	27

	Total Hexagons	Blank Hexagons	Shaded Hexagons
Row 27	28	26	2
Row 28	29	25	4
Row 29	30	24	6

Challenge: The next four rows in which only shaded hexagons appear are 53, 80, 161, and 242.

Chapter 5

p. 91

Number of Equally Spaced Points n	Degree Measure of Each Central Angle $\dfrac{360°}{n}$	Possible Values for r Such That $r<n$ and r and n Are Relatively Prime	Number of Different Star Polygons
5	72°	1,2,3,4	2
6	60°	1,5	1
7	$51\frac{3}{7}°$ or 51.43°	1 to 6	3
8	45°	1,3,5,7	2
9	40°	1,2,4,5,7,8	3
10	36°	1,3,7,9	2
11	$32\frac{8}{11}°$ or 32.73°	1 to 10	5
12	30°	1,5,7,11	2
13	$27\frac{9}{13}°$ or 27.69°	1 to 12	6

p. 92

1. $\dfrac{n-1}{2}$

2. Find all numbers from 1 to n-1 that are relatively prime to n. Let x be the number of these. Then $x \div 2$ is the number of different star polygons.

Example: Suppose $n = 10$. There are four numbers relatively prime to 10: 1, 3, 7, and 9. Hence there are two different star polygons, because $4 \div 2 = 2$.

3. a. (0,0) (1,4) (2,3)

   b. (0,0) (1,5) (2,4) (3,3)

   c. (0,0) (1,6) (2,5) (3,4)

   d. (0,0) (1,10) (2,9) (3,8) (4,7) (5,6)

   e. (0,0) (1,11) (2,10) (3,9) (4,8) (5,7) (6,6)

   f. (0,0) (1,12) (2,11) (3,10) (4,9) (5,8) (6,7)

4. They are the same.

5. None are different.

p. 95

	{n / r}	Degree Measure of Inscribed Angle		{n / r}	Degree Measure of Inscribed Angle
a.	{4 / 1}	90°	b.	{5 / 1}	108°
c.	{5 / 2}	36°	d.	{6 / 1}	120°
e.	{7 / 1}	128.57°	f.	{7 / 2}	77.14°
g.	{7 / 3}	25.71°	h.	{8 / 1}	135°
i.	{8 / 3}	45°	j.	{9 / 1}	140°
k.	{9 / 2}	100°	l.	{10 / 1}	144°
m.	{10 / 3}	72°	n.	{11 / 1}	147.27°
o.	{n / 1}	$\dfrac{180°(n-2)}{n}$			

Challenge: Each arc of the circle in $\{n / r\}$ has degree measure $360° \div n$ and thus the inscribed angle intercepting that arc has degree measure $\frac{1}{2} \times \frac{360°}{n}$. The number of arcs intercepted by the inscribed angle formed by the chords at any point of a star polygon $\{n / r\}$ is $|n - 2r|$. Therefore, each inscribed angle of $\{n / r\}$ has degree measure $|n - 2r| \frac{360°}{2n} = |n - 2r| \frac{180°}{n}$.

p. 97

Number of Equally Spaced Points n	Possible Values for r Such That r<n and r and n Are Not Relatively Prime	Number of Different Modified Star Polygons
6	2,3,4	2
8	2,4,6	2
9	3,6	1
10	2,4,5,6,8	3
12	2,3,4,6,8,9,10	4
25	5,10,15,20	2

p. 106

5. No.
   a. (1,1) (2,4) (3,5) (6,6)
   b. (1,1) (2,6) (3,4) (5,9)   (7,8) (10,10)
   c. (1,1) (2,7) (3,9) (4,10)   (5,8) (6,11)   (12,12)
   d. (1,1) (3,3) (5,5) (7,7)
   e. (1,1) (2,5) (4,7) (8,8)
   f. (1,1) (5,5) (7,7) (11,11)

6. The product designs $[n,a]$ and $[n,b]$, where $a \times b = 1$ in mod n, are the same.

7. a. 1 line
   b. 1 line
   c. 1 line
   d. 1 line
   e. 2 lines
   f. 1 line
   g. 1 line
   h. 1 line
   i. 1 line
   j. 1 line
   k. 1 line
   l. 2 lines

169

Chapter 8

Table 1
90° Spirograms, Natural Numbers

Spirogram	Order	Basic Pattern	Return to S? Yes	Return to S? No	Number of Repetitions of Basic Pattern
90°S₁	1	1	X		4
90°S₁,₂	2	1-2	X		2
90°S₁,₂,₃	3	1-2-3	X		4
90°S₁,₂,₃,₄	4	1-2-3-4		X	does not return
90°S₁,₂,...,₅	5	1-2-3-4-5	X		4
90°S₁,₂,...,₆	6	1-2-3-4-5-6	X		2
90°S₁,₂,...,₇	7	1-2-3-4-5-6-7	X		4
90°S₁,₂,...,₈	8	1-2-3-4-5-6-78		X	does not return

3. Give the order of those spirograms which do not return to the starting point S. 4,8

Table 2
90° Spirograms, Odd Numbers

Spirogram	Order	Basic Pattern	Return to S? Yes	Return to S? No	Number of Repetitions of Basic Pattern
90°S₁	1	1	X		4
90°S₁,₃	2	1-3	X		2
90°S₁,₃,₅	3	1-3-5	X		4
90°S₁,₃,₅,₇	4	1-3-5-7		X	does not return
90°S₁,₃,₅,...,₉	5	1-3-5-7-9	X		4
90°S₁,₃,₅,...,₁₁	6	1-3-5-7-9-11	X		2
90°S₁,₃,₅,...,₁₃	7	1-3-5-7-9-11-13	X		4

3. Give the order of those spirograms which do not return to the starting point S. 4

Table 3
90° Spirograms, Even Numbers

Spirogram	Order	Basic Pattern	Return to S? Yes	Return to S? No	Number of Repetitions of Basic Pattern
90°S₂	1	2	X		4
90°S₂,₄	2	2-4	X		2
90°S₂,₄,₆	3	2-4-6	X		4
90°S₂,₄,₆,₈	4	2-4-6-8		X	does not return
90°S₂,₄,₆,...,₁₀	5	2-4-6-8-10	X		4
90°S₂,₄,₆,...,₁₂	6	2-4-6-8-10-12	X		2
90°S₂,₄,₆,...,₁₄	7	2-4-6-8-10-12-14	X		4

3. Give the order of those spirograms which do not return to the starting point S. 4

Table 4
90° Spirograms, Fibonacci Numbers

Spirogram	Order	Basic Pattern	Return to S? Yes	Return to S? No	Number of Repetitions of Basic Pattern
90°S₁	1	1	X		2
90°S₁,₁,₂	3	1-1-2	X		4
90°S₁,₁,₂,₃	4	1-1-2-3		X	does not return
90°S₁,₁,₂,₃,₅	5	1-1-2-3-5	X		4
90°S₁,₁,₂,₃,₅,₈	6	1-1-2-3-5-8	X		2
90°S₁,₁,₂,₃,₅,₈,₁₃	7	1-1-2-3-5-8-13	X		4

3. Give the order of those spirograms which do not return to the starting point S. 4

Table 5
60° Spirograms, Natural Numbers

Spirogram	Order	Basic Pattern	Return to S? Yes	Return to S? No	Number of Repetitions of Basic Pattern
60°S₁	1	1	X		6
60°S₁,₂	2	1-2	X		3
60°S₁,₂,₃	3	1-2-3	X		2
60°S₁,₂,₃,₄	4	1-2-3-4	X		3
60°S₁,₂,...,₅	5	1-2-3-4-5	X		6
60°S₁,₂,...,₆	6	1-2-3-4-5-6		X	does not return
60°S₁,₂,...,₇	7	1-2-3-4-5-6-7	X		6
60°S₁,₂,...,₈	8	1-2-3-4-5-6-7-8	X		3

2. Give the order of those spirograms which do not return to the starting point S. 6

Table 6
60° Spirograms, Odd Numbers

Spirogram	Order	Basic Pattern	Return to S? Yes	Return to S? No	Number of Repetitions of Basic Pattern
60°S₁	1	1	X		6
60°S₁,₃	2	1-3	X		3
60°S₁,₃,₅	3	1-3-5	X		2
60°S₁,₃,₅,₇	4	1-3-5-7	X		3
60°S₁,₃,₅,...,₉	5	1-3-5-7-9	X		6
60°S₁,₃,₅,...,₁₁	6	1-3-5-7-9-11		X	does not return

4. Give the order of those spirograms which do not return to the starting point S. 6

Table 7
60° Spirograms, Even Numbers

Spirogram	Order	Basic Pattern	Return to S? Yes	Return to S? No	Number of Repetitions of Basic Pattern
60°S₂	1	2	X		6
60°S₂,₄	2	2-4	X		3
60°S₂,₄,₆	3	2-4-6	X		2
60°S₂,₄,₆,₈	4	2-4-6-8	X		3
60°S₂,₄,₆,...,₁₀	5	2-4-6-8-10	X		6
60°S₂,₄,₆,...,₁₂	6	2-4-6-8-10-12		X	does not return

2. Give the order of those spirograms which do not return to the starting point S. 6

Table 8
60° Spirograms, Fibonacci Numbers

Spirogram	Order	Basic Pattern	Return to S? Yes	Return to S? No	Number of Repetitions of Basic Pattern
60°S₁	1	1	X		6
60°S₁,₁,₂	3	1-1-2	X		2
60°S₁,₁,₂,₃	4	1-1-2-3	X		3
60°S₁,₁,₂,₃,₅	5	1-1-2-3-5	X		6
60°S₁,₁,₂,₃,₅,₈	6	1-1-2-3-5-8		X	does not return
60°S₁,₁,₂,₃,₅,₈,₁₃	7	1-1-2-3-5-8-13	X		6

4. Give the order of those spirograms which do not return to the starting point S. 6

Chapter 8

Table 9
120° Spirograms, Natural Numbers

Spirogram	Order	Basic Pattern	Return to S? Yes	Return to S? No	Number of Repetitions of Basic Pattern
$120°S_1$	1	1	X		3
$120°S_{1,2}$	2	1-2	X		3
$120°S_{1,2,3}$	3	1-2-3		X	does not return
$120°S_{1,2,3,4}$	4	1-2-3-4	X		3
$120°S_{1,2,\ldots,5}$	5	1-2-3-4-5	X		3
$120°S_{1,2,\ldots,6}$	6	1-2-3-4-5-6		X	does not return
$120°S_{1,2,\ldots,7}$	7	1-2-3-4-5-6-7	X		3
$120°S_{1,2,\ldots,8}$	8	1-2-3-4-5-6-7-8	X		3

2. Give the order of those spirograms which do not return to the starting point S. **3, 6**

Table 10
120° Spirograms, Odd Numbers

Spirogram	Order	Basic Pattern	Return to S? Yes	Return to S? No	Number of Repetitions of Basic Pattern
$120°S_1$	1	1	X		3
$120°S_{1,3}$	2	1-3	X		3
$120°S_{1,3,5}$	3	1-3-5		X	does not return
$120°S_{1,3,5,7}$	4	1-3-5-7	X		3
$120°S_{1,3,5,\ldots,9}$	5	1-3-5-7-9	X		3
$120°S_{1,3,5,\ldots,11}$	6	1-3-5-7-9-11		X	does not return

4. Give the order of those spirograms which do not return to the starting point S. **3, 6**

Table 11
120° Spirograms, Even Numbers

Spirogram	Order	Basic Pattern	Return to S? Yes	Return to S? No	Number of Repetitions of Basic Pattern
$120°S_2$	1	2	X		3
$120°S_{2,4}$	2	2-4	X		3
$120°S_{2,4,6}$	3	2-4-6		X	does not return
$120°S_{2,4,6,8}$	4	2-4-6-8	X		3
$120°S_{2,4,6,\ldots,10}$	5	2-4-6-8-10	X		3
$120°S_{2,4,6,\ldots,12}$	6	2-4-6-8-10-12		X	does not return

2. Give the order of those spirograms which do not return to the starting point S. **3, 6**

Table 12
120° Spirograms, Fibonacci Numbers

Spirogram	Order	Basic Pattern	Return to S? Yes	Return to S? No	Number of Repetitions of Basic Pattern
$120°S_1$	1	1	X		3
$120°S_{1,1,2}$	3	1-1-2		X	does not return
$120°S_{1,1,2,3}$	4	1-1-2-3	X		3
$120°S_{1,1,2,3,5}$	5	1-1-2-3-6	X		3
$120°S_{1,1,2,3,5,8}$	6	1-1-2-3-5-8		X	does not return
$120°S_{1,1,2,3,5,8,13}$	7	1-1-2-3-5-8-13	X		3

4. Give the order of those spirograms which do not return to the starting point S. **3, 6**

Table 13
Orders of Open Spirograms

For the turns listed below, no closed figure is obtained if the order number is in the sequence listed below.	
Turns	Order Number Sequence
90°	4, 8, *12, 16,* ..., *4n*
60°	6, *12, 18, 24,* ..., *6n*
120°	3, *6, 9, 12,* ..., *3n*

Table 14
Repetition Factors and Orders of Closed Spirograms

90° Spirograms:

Repetition factor is *two* if the order is in the sequence **2, 6, 10** ..., **(4n-2)**
Repetition factor is *four* if the order is in the sequence **1, 3, 5,** ..., **(2n-1)**

60° Spirograms:

Repetition factor is *two* if the order is in the sequence **3, 9, 15, 21, 27,** ...
Repetition factor is *three* if the order is in the sequence **2, 4, 8, 10, 14, 16, 20, 22,** ...
Repetition factor is *four* if the order is in the sequence **1, 5, 7, 11, 13, 17, 19, 23,** ...

120° Spirograms:

Repetition factor is *three* if the order is in the sequence **1, 2, 4, 5, 7, 8, 10, 11** ...

171

BIBLIOGRAPHY

Albarn, Keith, el al. *The Language of Pattern*. New York: Harper and
Row, Publishers, 1974.

Benson, William H., and Jacoby, Oswald. *New Recreations with Magic
Squares*. New York: Dover Publications, Inc., 1976.

Bezuszka, Stanley; Kenney, Margaret; and Silvey, Linda. *Tessellations:
The Geometry of Patterns*. Palo Alto, California: Creative
Publications, Inc., 1977.

Bourgoin, J. *Arabic Geometrical Pattern and Design*. New York: Dover
Publications, Inc., 1973.

Bragdon, Claude F. *Frozen Fountain*. New York: Knopf Publishing
Company, 1932.

Bruni, James V., and Silverman, Helene J. "Let's Do It—Making
Patterns With a Square." *Arithmetic Teacher*, Vol. 24 (April 1977), pp.
265-272.

Coxeter, H.S.M. *Introduction to Geometry*. New York: John Wiley and
Sons, Inc., 1961.

Duncan, David, and Litwiller, Bonnie. "A Pattern: Pascal's Triangle
and Prime Numbers." *Mathematics Teacher*, Vol. 68 (January 1975),
pp. 23-26.

Eves, Howard. *A Survey of Geometry*, Volume 1. Boston: Allyn and
Bacon, Inc., 1963.

Elliott, H.A.; MacLean, James R.; and Jorden, Janet M. *Geometry in the
Classroom: New Concepts and Methods*. Canada: Holt, Rinehart, and
Winston, 1968.

Forseth, Sonia. *Math Art Posters*. Palo Alto, California: Creative
Publications, Inc., 1973.

-----, and Troutman, Andria Price. "Designs Exhibiting Mathematical
Structures." *School Science and Mathematics*, Vol. 64 (December
1974), pp. 701-708.

-----. "Using Mathematical Structures to Generate Artistic Designs."
Mathematics Teacher, Vol. 67 (May 1974), pp. 393-398.

Gardner, Martin. "Mathematical Games." *Scientific American*, Vol. 266
(December 1966), pp. 128-132.

Gillon, Edmund V., Jr. *Geometric Design and Ornament*. New York:
Dover Publications, Inc., 1969.

Hilton, A.J.W. "On Double Diagonal and Cross Latin Squares." *Journal
of the London Mathematical Society*, Vol. 6 (June 1973), Second Series,
pp. 679-689.

Hornung, Clarence P. *Allover Pattern for Designers and Craftsmen*. New York: Dover Publications, Inc., 1975.

Hughes, Barnabas. *Thinking Through Problems*. Palo Alto, California: Creative Publications, Inc., 1976.

Johnson, Martin L. "Generating Patterns from Transformations." *Arithmetic Teacher*, Vol. 24 (March 1977), pp. 191-195.

Kepes, Gyorgy. *Module Proportion Symmetry Rhythm*. New York: George Braziller, Inc., 1966.

Lettau, John. *Graph Paper Designs*. Santa Maria, California: L and M Educational Enterprises, 1972.

Loeb, Arthur L. *Color and Symmetry*. New York: John Wiley and Sons, Inc., 1971.

Odds, Frank. "Spirolaterals." *Mathematics Teacher*, Vol. 66 (February 1973), pp. 121-124.

Ranucci, Ernest. *Seeing Shapes*. Palo Alto, California: Creative Publications, Inc., 1973.

Stevens, Peter S. *Patterns in Nature*. Boston: Little, Brown and Company, 1974.

Troutman, Andria, and Forseth, Sonia. *Math Art Posters Teacher's Guide*. Palo Alto, California: Creative Publications, Inc., 1973.

Wong, Wucius. *Principles of Two-Dimensional Design*. New York: Van Nostrand and Reinhold Company, 1972.

APPENDIX

TABULAR DESIGN GRID FOR 8 × 8 AND SMALLER TABLES

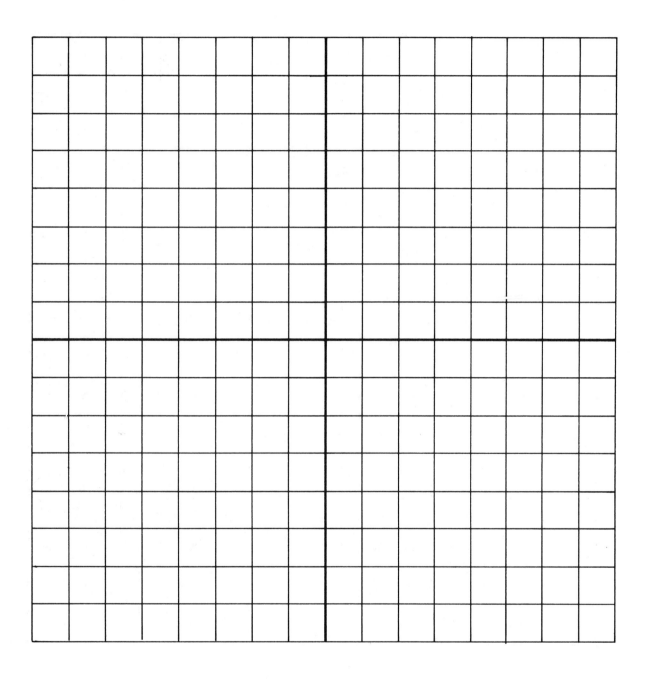

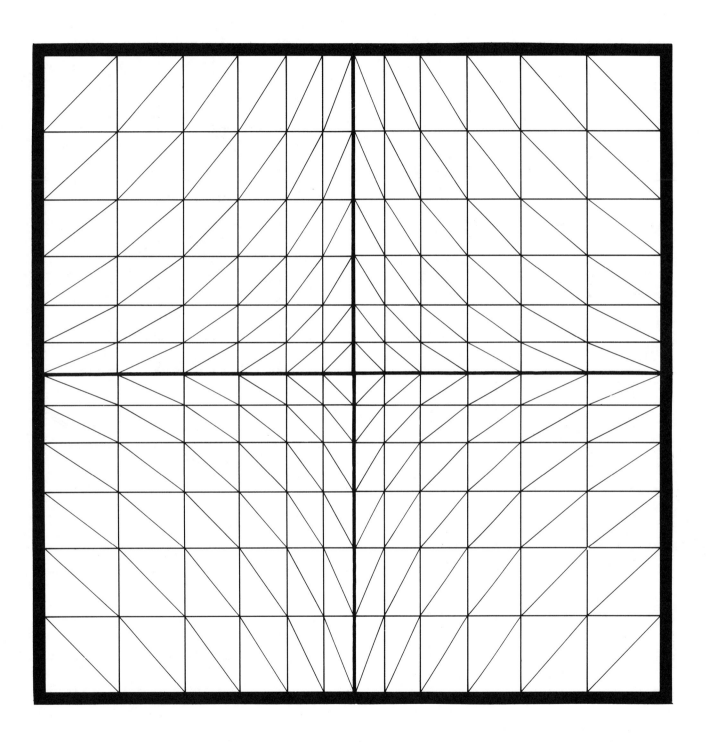

TABULAR DESIGN GRID FOR 6 × 6 AND SMALLER TABLES

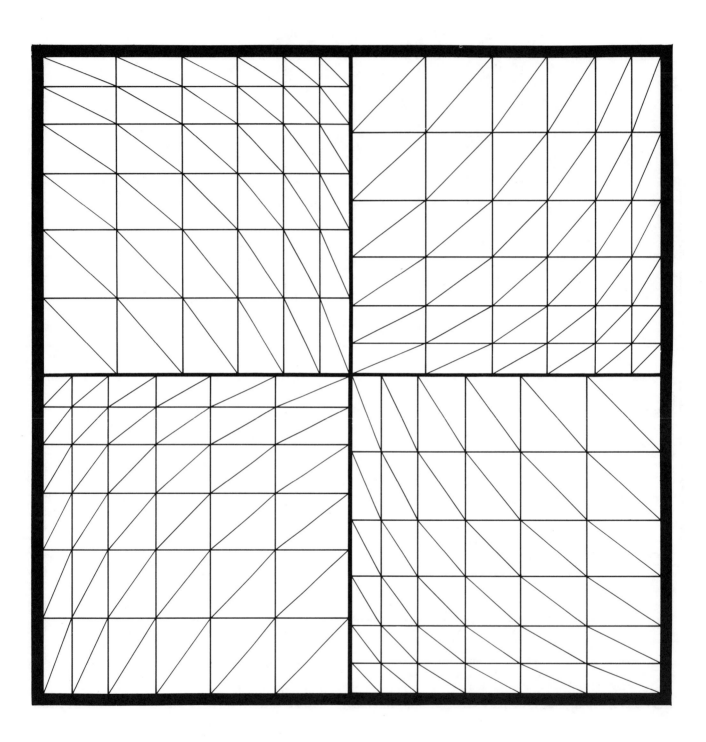

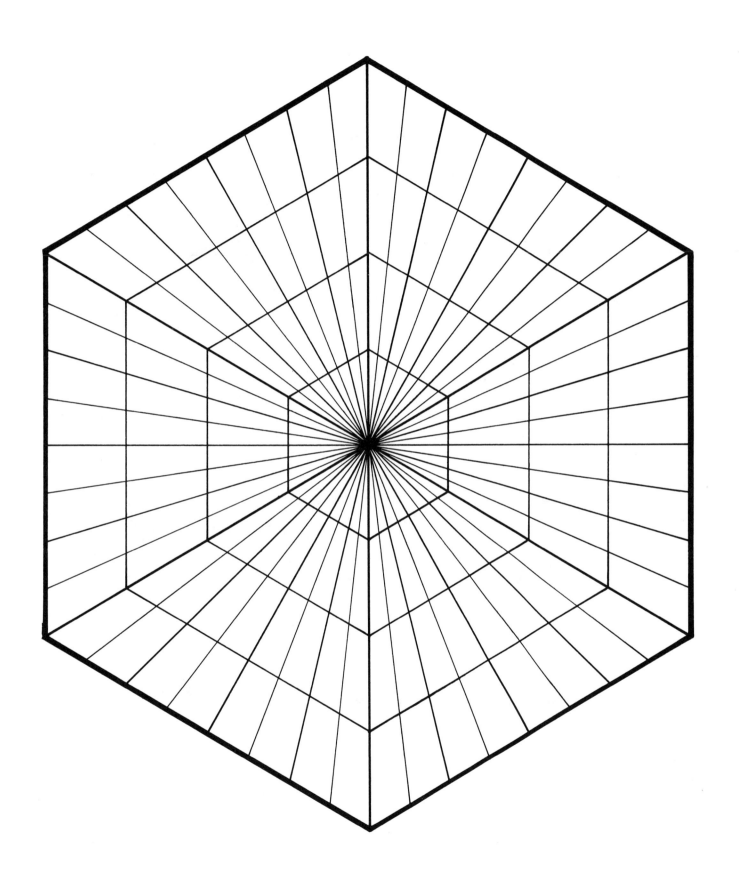

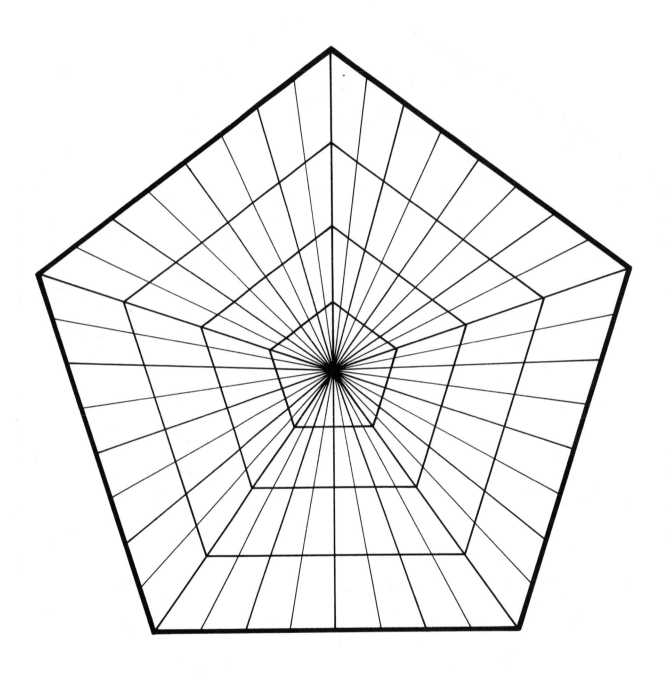

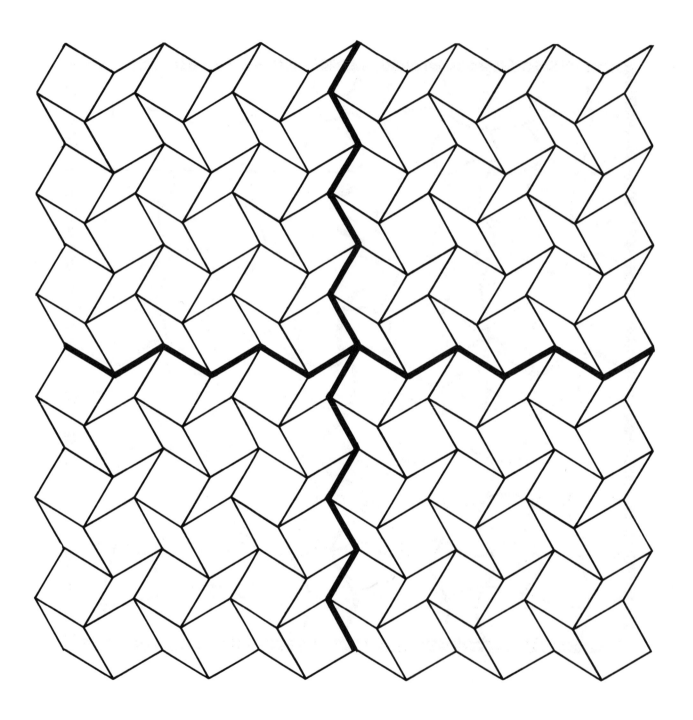

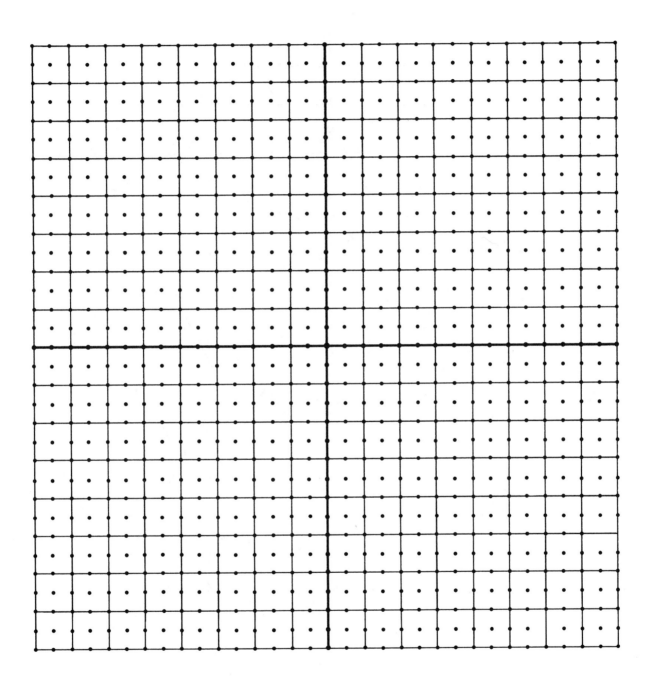

PASCAL'S TRIANGLE DESIGN GRID—
TESSELLATION OF REGULAR TRIANGLES AND HEXAGONS

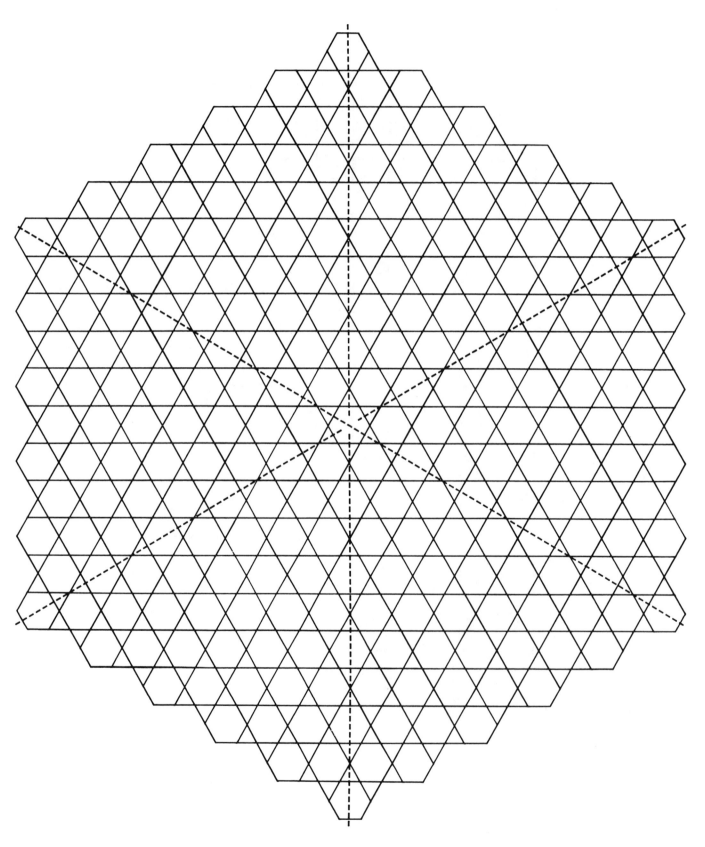

A-10

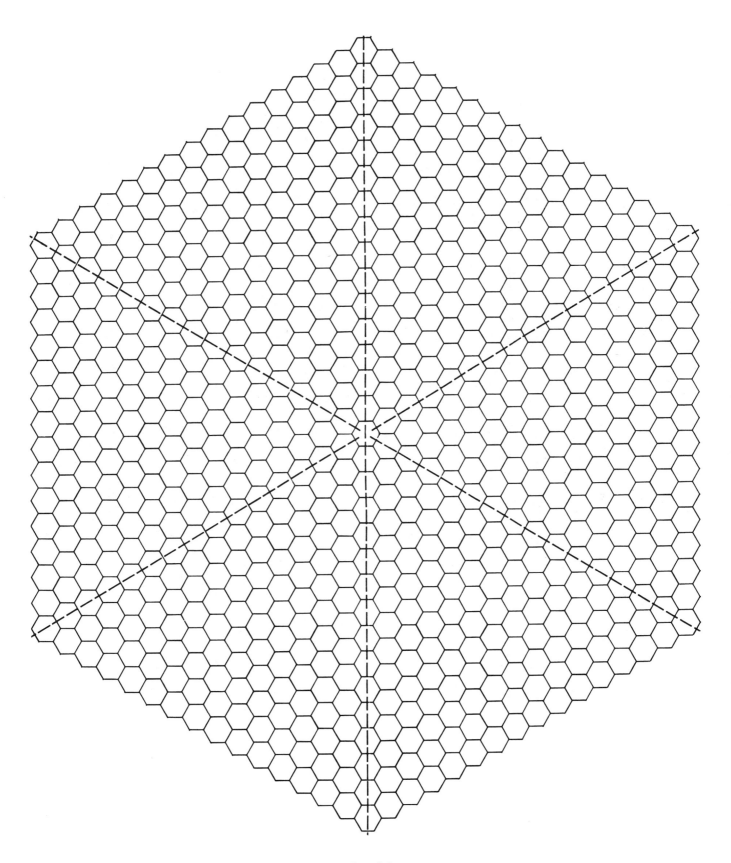

A–11

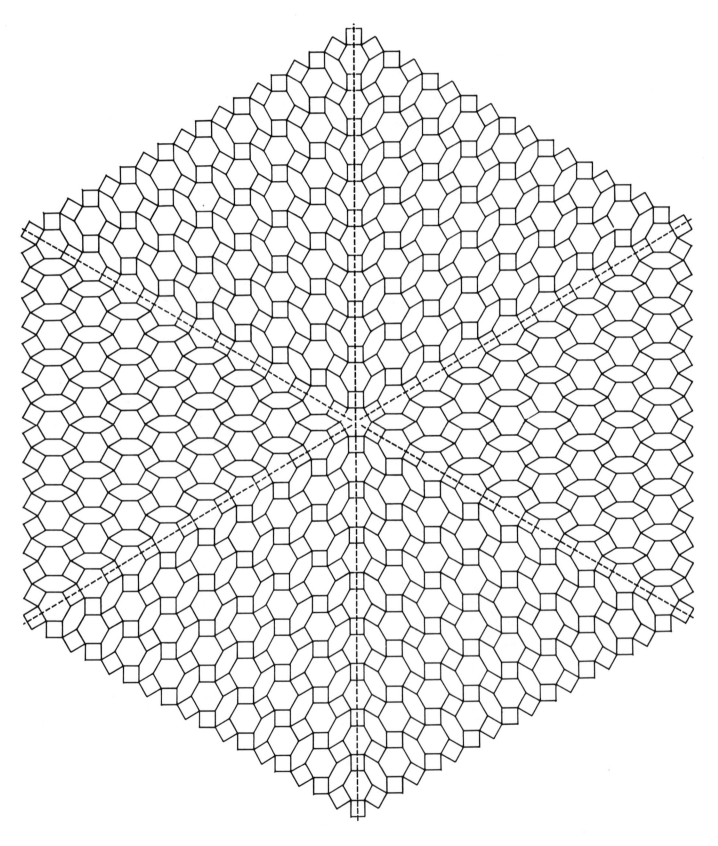

A–12

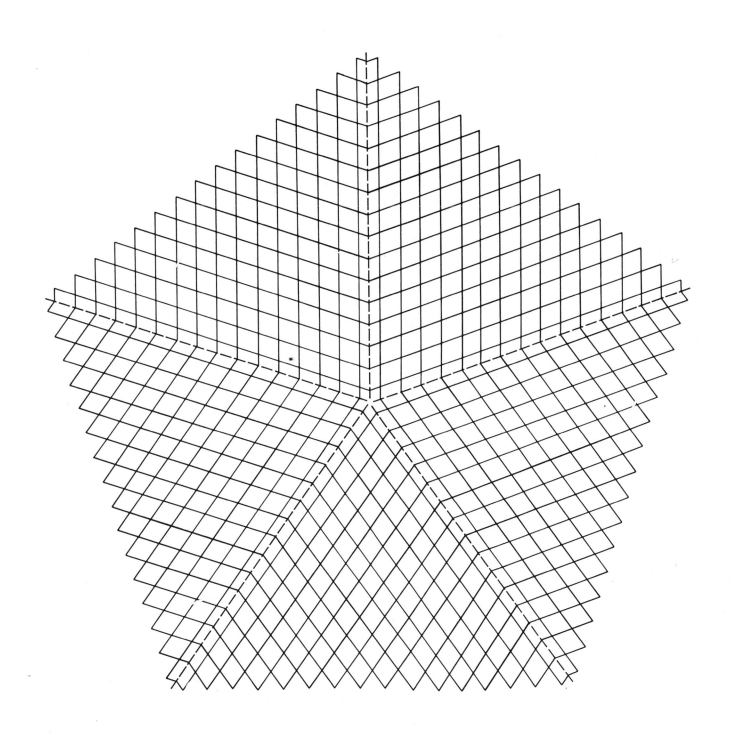

TESSELLATION OF 60°–120° RHOMBI

A–18

GRID OF SQUARES

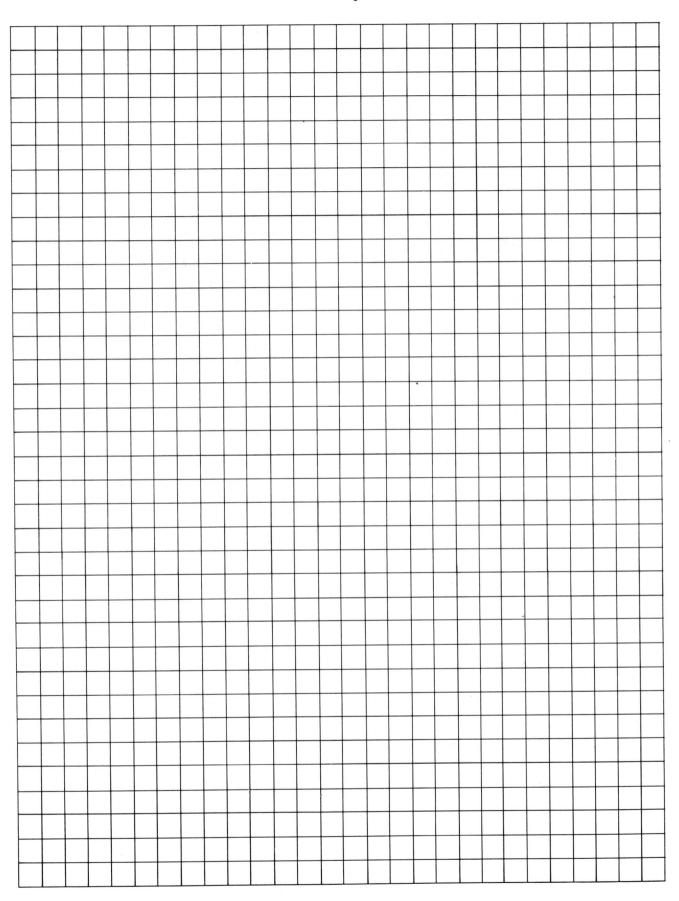

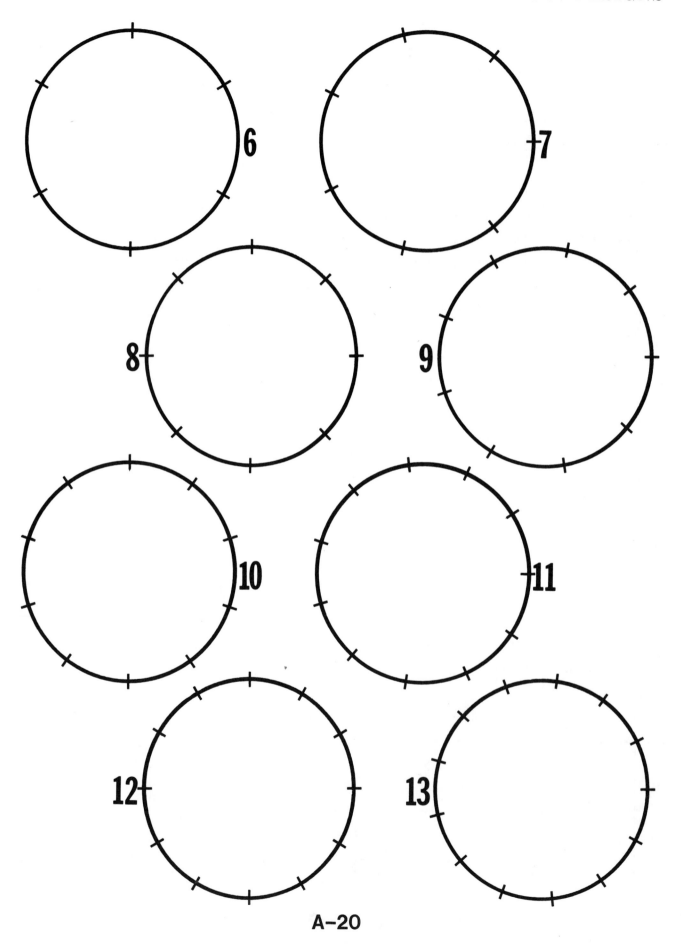

SQUARE DOT PAPER FOR MAGIC SQUARE DESIGNS

A-21

ISOMETRIC DOT PAPER FOR SPIROGRAMS

ISOMETRIC DOT PAPER FOR SPIROGRAMS

SQUARE DOT PAPER FOR SPIROGRAMS

SQUARE DOT PAPER FOR SPIROGRAMS

NOTES

NOTES

NOTES

NOTES